SMELLORAMA!

Nose games for dogs

D1604963

Viviane Theby

Hubble & Hattie

Hubble & Hattie

For more than eighteen years, the folk at Veloce have concentrated their publishing efforts on all-things automotive. Now, in a break with tradition, the company launches a new imprint for a new publishing genre!

The Hubble & Hattie imprint – so-called in memory of two, dearly-loved West Highland Terriers – will be the home of a range of books that cover all things animal, all produced to the same high quality of content and presentation as our motoring books, and offering the same great value for money.

www.hubbleandhattie.com

First published in February 2010 by Veloce Publishing Limited, Veloce House, Parkway Farm Business Park, Middle Farm Way, Poundbury, Dorchester, DT1 3AR, England.
Fax 01305 250479/e-mail: info@hubbleandhattie.com/web: www.hubbleandhattie.com.
ISBN: 978-1-845842-93-2 UPC: 6-36847-04293-6
Original publication © 2009 Kynos Verlag, Dr Dieter Fleig GmbH. www.kynos-verlag.de
Readers with ideas for books about animals, or animal-related topics, are invited to write to the editorial director of Veloce Publishing at the above address.
British Library Cataloguing in Publication Data – A catalogue record for this book is available from the British Library. Typesetting, design and page make-up all by Veloce Publishing Ltd on Apple Mac. Printed in India by Imprint Digital.

CONTENTS

LET'S GO!

PREFACE

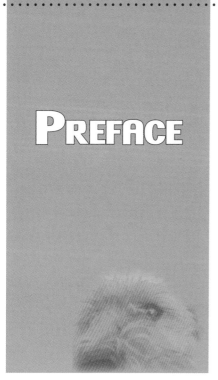

Most of our dogs want to work; they have been bred for this purpose for many, many years. And most people have fun working with their dog. However, often they lack the right ideas to do this, or there is not enough time to go to a dog training class, especially if it's some distance away. But it doesn't have to be like this as there are many fascinating things that you can train your dog to do at home, which is clearly more important than going to a training class once a week.

Very often we invite our dogs into our world during training, or while playing small games. They learn tricks, perfect obedience or jumping over obstacles; things they would not do by themselves. This can be very entertaining for them, as long as the training methods are kind.

By way of this book I would like to give you the opportunity to experience the world of your dog. Try to imagine perceiving the environment through your nose for a change, as a dog does. This is very hard for us to envisage, but the feats that dogs are able to perform with their noses are absolutely fascinating and awe-inspiring!

In my time training rescue dogs I have often been impressed by these feats. Dogs are able to sweep through an entire building and find people inside in no time, or search large areas for missing persons.

Two incidents I learned about have especially impressed me. A colleague from a different locating team told me of a water rescue mission in which a diver had gone missing (in these missions the dog is taken onto the water in a boat to search for human scents). The dog indicated a location, from which — taking currents into account — a position was established where the diver was likely to be. Other divers went down, but found nothing. The dog was set on the trail a second time and indicated the exact same position again. The dog handler, who knew her dog very well, was certain that something was there. A special diving squad was summoned and eventually the drowned person was found; he was twenty metres below the surface and pretty much covered by mud! Although I had already learned a lot about a dog's fantastic sense of smell in my work with rescue dogs, this was still staggering: how could a dog detect that scent?

Another amazing story came from a French fire brigade dog handler, who told of dogs which, having been given an item belonging to a person to smell, would seek and find that person, even if they had walked straight through the city, for example over a market square full of people, over roads with busy

traffic, or similar. At the time, I could hardly conceive of this happening until I actually saw such a dog at work: truly unbelievable!

In the following chapters I would like to invite you to learn from your dog because, when it comes to the nose, he or she is by far superior to us. Apart from the fact that this superiority may be very entertaining for you and your dog, it also has practical value and use. Imagine that you lost your wedding ring in the grass at a garden party and your dog found it for you! Or maybe you are allergic to nuts and your dog can tell you if what you are about to eat contains them. Not possible, you think? But it is!

So, come with me into the fascinating world of your dog's nose. We may never be able to achieve the same things, but can still learn to appreciate it and its abilities, something that can only be beneficial to a good partnership between dog and human.

The following exercises can be performed by any dog unless it has lost its sense of smell. Your dog's breed or age are irrelevant. Let's go!

Viviane Theby

How does a dog's nose work?

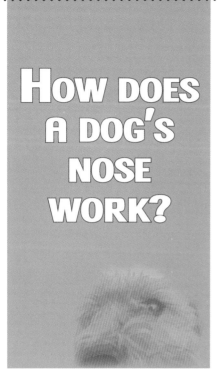

Let's take a closer look at how the dog's nose works, in order to better understand the scenting process.

In fact, a dog does not smell with her nose but with the olfactory epithelium, a thin mucous membrane layer which lines part of the nose cavity and which air breathed in streams past. Scent molecules in the air diffuse onto the mucous on this membrane and can then be perceived.

The olfactory epithelium consists of three different cell types. First, there are the support cells which create the basic structure, inside which are the actual olfactory receptor cells – nerve cells which connect directly to the brain. The third cell type are basal cells; actually, regrowing olfactory cells, because olfactory receptor cells grow continuously, die, and are replaced by new ones in a cycle of one to two months. This means that olfactory receptor cells are the only nerve cells which are continuously replaced during an entire lifetime.

The olfactory cells have something resembling small antennae which grow into the mucous layer on the epithelium. Among other things, this mucous layer also contains antibodies which serve a very important function here, as the olfactory receptor cells represent a direct connection to the brain, which could be used as an entrance by a number of pathogens. It is in this mucous layer that the scent particles are dissolved. They bond with certain proteins in the membrane of the small antennae that grow into the mucous layer. A chemical reaction produces an electric potential which relays the information via the olfactory nerve to the brain. Although not certain, it appears that each olfactory cell features receptors – 'docking places' – for a single, specific scent: some 1000 different genes for different receptor cells in the olfactory epithelium have already been identified.

Whilst the total surface area of the human mucous membrane is $10cm^2$, that of a dog is around $170cm^2$. And a dog has over a hundred times more single olfactory cells in each square cm than does a human.

Another big difference is the size of the olfactory centre in the brain, which, in the dog, is proportionally much larger than in a human. The olfactory centre processes the information relayed from the olfactory epithelium, and actual differentiation between scents takes place. There are also many connections between the olfactory centre and many other parts of the brain connected with emotions or memory.

The smelling process itself is extremely interesting and far from having been researched in detail. In contrast to us, dogs are able to smell in 'stereo.' This means that they can individually process olfactory information from both nostrils, and thus are able to determine direction. If a dog finds a track, she knows in which direction that human or dog has walked; after all, for a natural predator like the dog, it would be very unfortunate indeed if she followed a trail in the wrong direction! Therefore, the common misconception that a dog first has to learn to follow a track in the right direction is just that.

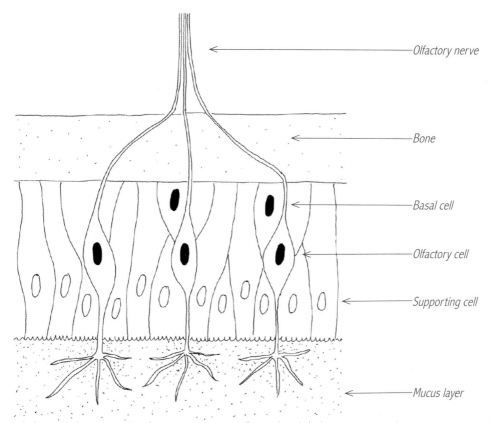

Olfactory nerve

Bone

Basal cell

Olfactory cell

Supporting cell

Mucus layer

A dog can also ascertain where a scent comes from when it belongs to a certain scent source, such as explosives for a dog trained to seek these. Much like we are able to determine the source of a sound, a dog can do something similar with scent.

The much more effective connections in the dog's olfactory centre also allow for a much higher resolution of the scent. This can easily be compared to digital photography. If the camera has a small imaging capacity, corresponding to the small olfactory centre of the human, image resolution will be very low, and details are likely to be out of focus. However, if the camera has a large imaging capacity, like the olfactory centre of the dog, then resolution will be higher and include much more detail.

We can only imagine what this is like for a dog. If we enter a room with an unpleasant smell, we note a mixture of scents, but are hardly ever able to differentiate between them. The dog, on the other hand, perceives an entire range of different, separate scents. Even if one specific scent is very dominant, a dog is still able to determine another, much fainter scent.

The function of the nose, as noted here, clarifies a few things for our practical work. The mucous membrane in the nose, for example, should always be nice and wet to allow the scent particles to dissolve on it, especially in warm weather, which means that your dog should be offered water regularly, otherwise her ability to smell could suffer. A dog is only able to smell if she breathes in and lets air flow over the olfactory mucous membrane. This may sound simple and obvious; after all, a dog breathes all the time. However, remember that if a dog holds her breath at the specific moment that a scent is presented to her, she cannot be expected to have actually perceived the scent.

SMELLORAMA! *Nose games for dogs*

THE SENSE OF SMELL

So, what are these scent particles? What is it that the dog smells when, for example, she is following a trail?

Scent particles are chemical substances that exist in the environment which may be perceived by any living creature. Even single-cell organisms are able to locate certain chemical substances. The sense of smell is mainly necessary to find vital resources for the body and to preserve it from harmful substances.

These vital resources include sustenance – for example prey or water – but also social partners necessary for protected communal living and, most importantly, for procreation.

It is still strongly debated what it is exactly that a dog smells when she is trailing a human. It could be molecules given off from the body, or decomposition products. A human will lose approximately 40,000 old skin cells per minute, which are loaded with bacteria; bacteria is spread over our entire skin surface, several thousand, or possibly millions, per square centimetre. So one dead skin cell will provide food for the two or three bacteria upon it. This results in metabolic products, such as gases that become part of the scent.

Then, of course, the lessons that a dog is taught are also important. In pure tracking, the dog should follow the trail precisely, the thinking behind which is that she can smell the disturbance in the ground, ie: those compounds that are created when micro-organisms or plant parts die, or when they decompose due to bacteria. Some experiments that have been carried out whilst tracking various people seem to confirm this. However, my own view is that this is unnatural for the dog, and restricts her work, apparently to make it easier for the human, who then knows where the footprints are but not where the scent is that helps the dog orientate.

A great deal has been discovered about how dogs or other animals communicate with certain scents; so-called pheromones. For each species, an entire range of pheromones are used to transmit very many signals. These pheromones can provide detailed information on, for example, gender, age and mood of the individual who emits them. These concepts apply to communication within one species: even we humans transmit a number of different signals via pheromones of which we are completely unaware.

It is not beneficial for the dog to restrict herself to scents emanating from disturbance to the ground, when she is able to receive much more information, especially as a dog, in most cases, is well socialised with humans and is familiar with – and probably even knows the meaning of – human pheromones. All cells contain certain protein molecules that allow the body to differentiate between its 'own' and foreign. A dog can smell this also.

Of course, this is purely speculation which cannot be proved until the entire brain has been mapped with regard to the perception of certain scents. The aforementioned protein molecules, for example, are determined genetically, and are therefore different within individuals. It has been proven that bloodhounds have difficulty distinguishing between identical twins, but not non-identical ones.

I would like to describe a model that will help us imagine a scent on a track. Most behavioural patterns that a dog will display whilst on a track can be explained well in this way. This is only a model, but it is rather useful as it can help us put ourselves in our dog's place while he is working. The objective is to determine what the dog actually perceives, and we can try and imagine this based on our sense of sight. One person might prefer to look people in the eye and will best remember those who meet their gaze; another might prefer to observe someone's stature and is better able to remember that. Everybody at some point has looked at a small child and decided that he or she most closely resembles the father or the mother. Which parent they choose depends on what it is that the person perceives first – eyes, nose, mouth, etc – when viewing a face.

To a dog, every human gives off an individual scent, and I speculated earlier about what this may consist of. In the end, however, this is not important as a dog will most likely perceive many different scents which combine to provide one rather complex image. In an effort to illustrate this point, imagine a person standing

When standing, a person emanates a spherical scent cloud ...

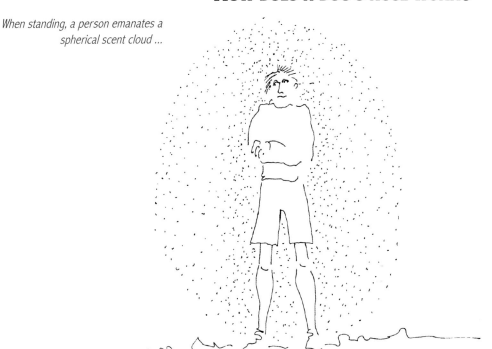

... but once moving, this becomes a scent tunnel.

9

still in one place. The scent molecules given off diffuse into the surrounding air, forming a circle – a spherical scent cloud – around the person. If the person moves, the scent sphere is transformed into a scent tube. This scent tube, of course, changes and evolves, much like the condensation trail of an aeroplane. Some of the scent particles will disperse, some will sink to the ground, which explains why, if the scent is fresh, some dogs will walk with their nose high in the air. They do not need to sniff the ground, as they are walking through a tunnel of scent molecules. The older the scent, the lower the dog usually holds his nose, as scent particles will gradually sink to the ground.

However, the level at which the scent particles are does not only depend on the trail's freshness, but also on air movement. Wind will deflect the scent tube from its original path, requiring the dog to walk several metres to the side of the course that the person took, unless she is trained to follow ground disturbances. Strong wind can also damage our virtual scent tube. If there is a strong headwind, the dog may now and again lose the scent, though then later pick up faint shreds of scent. Of course, how the dog will react to this depends on her level of training and experience. If there's a strong sidewind, at a certain wind speed, the dog would be unable to follow a scent at all.

Warm air rises, and scent rises with it. If your dog is searching with her nose to the ground when in the shade, you may notice that she lifts her nose higher as soon as she enters a sunnier patch.

This model also explains why old scents are different from fresh ones. Scent particles decrease in quantity and also change in quality, and the more fleeting particles disappear as the others sink to the ground. The scenting ability of your dog will, in that case, also depend on how many different scents her scent image consists of.

In very sunny weather with hot, dry air, scent particles can spread through the air more easily, which means that they disappear faster than in humid weather (humidity, including dew, will preserve a scent to some extent), so, early morning or late evening are the best times of day to carry out a search. In training, however, you should try exercises in all possible weather conditions to better learn about your dog and her abilities.

In most cases you should let your dog work on her own. However, there are instances where human intellect is needed. It may be that your dog has caught the scent in question but doesn't know how to continue, in which case you will need to assess wind, weather and landscape conditions to enable your dog to continue the search in the right area.

Of course, your dog's work method will very much depend on what training she has received. A dog may learn, for example, to find a particular scent, as in the case of a dog trained in explosives location (or, in our search-and-find game, the scent of the toy), or she could learn to follow a given trail of scent. A dog can be trained to work with her nose to the ground (eg for tracking), with the nose half raised (eg to follow a scent), or with the nose high (eg to scan an area). These artificial distinctions are really just for our benefit: if left to her own devices, a dog will automatically use the method that she finds most effective.

However, a dog can be trained to carry out specific work in a certain way; for example, a dog trained to find narcotics and to indicate her findings. If she is shown narcotics again and again in the same container, it may be that, in training, she carries out her work impeccably, but 'fails' in a real case as she has only learned to find the *container* and not the narcotics inside.

We cannot *tell* the dog what to find, and can only attempt to make it clear through the training concept. For this reason it is important to know as much as possible about the learning process of your dog, as well as her sense of smell and all that is related to it. With this knowledge in mind, it is necessary to reconsider the training concept critically time and time again.

But now let us look at practical application.

Hide & Seek Games for Beginners

In the preface, I mentioned a few of the ways that dogs use their nose, and in this respect we do not need to, and actually can't, train them. However, what we do need to teach them is how to communicate what it is they are actually scenting. We have to be able to tell the dog what he has to smell for us, and must be able to recognise when he is on a 'hot' trail or has found something, which means that these things – as is so often the case in dog training – have first to be learned by the human.

Finding a lost item: how do I tell my dog?

We start very simply. Take one of your dog's toys and have him sit in the middle of the room (someone can hold him there if he's unlikely to stay). Place the toy in a corner of the room so that your dog can see it, and let him go with the command "Find!"

For dogs who are not crazy about toys, and who might look at you as if to say "You find it," you can use a treat, or a tin filled with something tasty, which you open for your dog once he has found it. "Found?" you may say, "He didn't even have to search!"

Don't forget that dogs cannot understand our language, so will not comprehend what is meant by "Find!" But, using this method, we can teach him relatively quickly. In the next step, the item to be found is placed behind an armchair or something similar, but still with the dog watching. Again, the dog is released with the command "Find!" (By the way, the actual command you use is up to you.)

Repeat this exercise two or three times in different spots so that sometimes the item might be behind the armchair, sometimes behind the waste-basket, or sometimes under a cushion.

Then lead your dog out of the room while you place the toy in one of the three previously used hiding places. Call your dog back into the room and, with your chosen command, allow him to begin the search (but avoid looking in the direction of the hiding place). Your dog may head for the three known hiding places one after the other, or may use his nose to locate the hidden item. Whichever is the case it's important to praise him enthusiastically when he finds the toy/treat, really letting him know how great you think it is. Often, what we regard as praise – such as bending over him in a dominant manner, and patting his head – is rather uncomfortable for your dog, so observe closely to see if what you are doing is really perceived as praise.

A very important factor in this respect is your voice. Learn to give your dog the highest praise! Please take this literally: it is actually important to use a high-pitched voice, as most dogs love this and those that don't can learn to.

Repeat this exercise until the item has been found in every one of the known hiding places at least once.

Then, at the point where your dog is enthusiastic and wanting more, it is time to stop; if he is signalling that he has had enough, the exercise has gone on too long. It is better to exercise several times a day, and only for a few minutes than to make a session too long. And it's also actually easier to build this into your daily routine as most people can find a spare three minutes at some point in their day.

RULE OF THUMB I

1. Always stop when it's still fun!

In the next session, start again by hiding the item with your dog watching, but this time in a different room. Walk to three different places, twice pretending that you are hiding something, and the last time actually doing so. Your dog has three hiding places to choose from: how does he decide which to go for? Does he use his nose and find the item immediately; does he go to the three spots just as you did; or does he begin to do so but then change course to walk straight to the item? At this point you can start to learn how to properly observe your dog. What does he look like when he smells something? How does he move his tail and ears in this situation? How does he react when he has found something?

Oh no, not AGAIN!

Now do the same thing again — with the three known hiding places — but without letting your dog see where you hide the toy or treat. Up to this point your dog should have understood the exercise, so if he is enthusiastically participating, searching and finding the hidden items, the time has come for the next step.

Hide the item without your dog watching, in an as yet unknown hiding place, but do not make it too difficult: at this stage of the training the target should be relatively easy to find.

Closely watch your dog: how does he react? Is his nose up in the air or does he sniff the ground? (You might find it helpful to video this stage in the proceedings and watch it later to study his body language.) He should be able to solve the problem with his nose, and, if he does, praise him as much as possible and end the training session.

I'd like to offer a little advice about the toy or the treats that you use. The toy should be used only in this searching game. At the end of the exercise it is put away and the dog should not be allowed to play with it at other times; this will make it more interesting for him to find. Be careful with giving food treats that you do not give too many; consider using part of your dog's daily ration instead so that there is no danger of over-feeding and allowing your dog to become overweight.

Perhaps "praise your dog" also needs a few words of explanation. The purpose of praise is to let your dog know and understand that he has done something extremely well: if you are able to make him grow an inch out of sheer pride, you will have succeeded.

Starting with the next training session, choose more and more difficult hiding places, ensuring always, though, that your dog can actually get to them. If he's not able to find the item, don't be tempted to help him, otherwise he may believe that you have a better sense of smell, and rely on your nose at some point in the future when you won't be able to help him.

Also pick hiding places at different heights from time to time; is he still able to locate the hidden toy or treat? Watch him closely! It's not necessary for you to correctly interpret every single movement that your

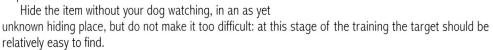

dog makes at this stage – after all, you know the hiding place – but if, in the future, you need to find something, the location of which you do not know (as is usually the case), then you have to be able to completely understand what your dog is doing and how he works. Is he still searching/ nearing the source of the scent? Has he caught the scent but cannot approach it, for whatever reason? You should be able to read all of this from your dog's actions.

Well done!

If your dog is able to find the toy or treats in the most difficult hiding places, try instructing him to "Find!" without hiding anything, and see at what point he abandons the search. (Only try this exercise if your dog has understood the concept completely and has solved complicated search tasks without turning to you for help.) How does he signal that there is nothing there? If he then looks at you, tries to make eye contact, or even return to you, praise him as if he had found something. This negative indication, as it is called, is just as important as if he *had* found something, as he is telling you that there is nothing to find. We will need this response again in the future, so carefully observe your dog and learn his reactions.

Don't carry out this negative indication exercise too often; as a general rule, maybe one out of thirty searches should be negative. So if you carry out one search each day, or two every two days, then you should have one negative indication per month, but not more.

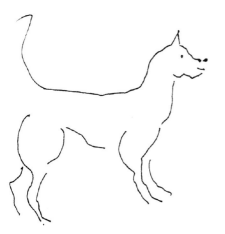

The right sort of praise should make your dog swell with pride!

SMELLORAMA! Nose games for dogs

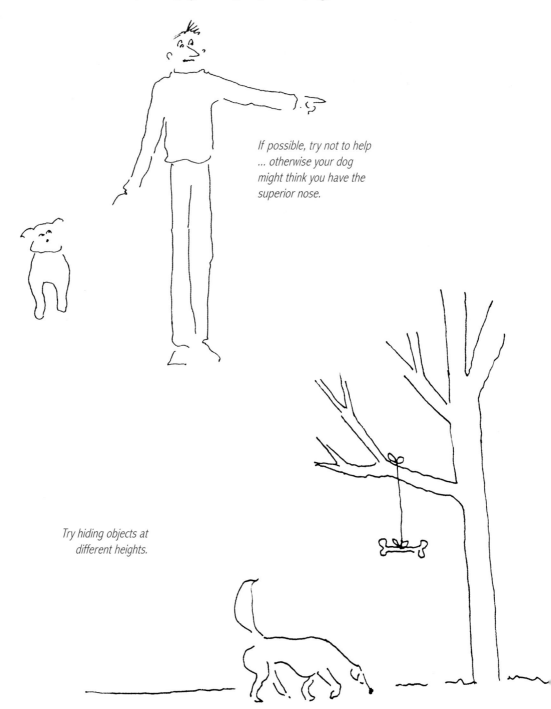

If possible, try not to help ... otherwise your dog might think you have the superior nose.

Try hiding objects at different heights.

Now you can move this game from the house to the garden, and maybe also let your dog find something on a walk. Initially, use the same toy or treats that your dog has been searching for in the house.

As you can see, we always move from something known towards something unknown, in very small steps, not because dogs are stupid, but because we don't have any other way to show them what we want. Once again: they do not understand our language, and it is up to us to find a way to communicate with them. If your dog fails to understand what you want, then the step was too large, and you should take smaller, intermediate steps.

RULES OF THUMB 2 AND 3

2: Always set up the exercise so that your dog is able to succeed
3: If possible, never repeat a successful exercise in exactly the same way

Initially, I place a lot of importance on these basic rules, which apply for any exercise, simply because I cannot mention every single possible situation in this book. I do, however, want to give you a chance to deal with these situations.

An explanation for rule of thumb number 2. Success is motivating, which, in itself, is a good reason to set up the exercise in a way that makes it possible for your dog to succeed. Success will increase his motivation to work with you. Also, this success is a means of communication for us. Just as we aren't able to tell the dog what we want him to do, he isn't able to tell us if he has correctly understood the exercise. If he has dealt with an exercise correctly, we get a good result; if he makes a mistake, this means he has not understood the task properly, or it was too difficult. You will have the most success with training if you are aware of and look for mistakes that *you* make, as these are the easiest to correct. We will carry out a small exercise later to exemplify this concept.

But first to explain rule of thumb number 3. An exercise should never be repeated in exactly the same way once the dog has understood it, the simple reason being that it is boring. Imagine a child at school — or maybe you can think back to your own time there. The teacher explains that an object falls because of something called gravity. If he was to repeat this single statement again and again all day, you would soon stop listening to him. But if he was to demonstrate this with several examples — once letting a stone drop out of his hand, once a feather — you would remain interested, and maybe understand some aspects that you hadn't thought about earlier. Our dogs, of course, feel similarly.

Constant repetition in exactly the same way is boring, and your dog will quickly lose interest. If you change the exercise slightly each time, it will make many things clearer to your dog.

Let's consider the simple command "Sit!" Constant monotonous repetition is much like a punishment at school where, for example, the line "I will be good in class" has to be written 50 times. However, instruction does need repetition, of course, so that your dog makes the connection in his brain and remembers it. Which brings us to —

RULE OF THUMB 4

4. Variation of the same exercise merely entails training in different places, with different distractions

It might be useful to actually write these rules (which are valid for all exercises and not just for scenting work) on a piece of paper that you can hang up where you and your dog usually train.

And now the exercise for you that I mentioned earlier. Whenever you want to teach your dog anything, it's important that you know exactly what it is you want. Let us take what we have attempted so far; that your dog find something which you, for example, have lost in the forest.

This is asking for too much!

Our exercise steps so far:

> Step 1: place an item (toy or treats) in front of your dog and let him locate it with the command "Find!"
> Step 2: hide the item with the dog watching you and again let him find it
> Step 3: the same exercise using two other hiding places
> Step 4: place the item in one of the three known hiding places without your dog watching
> Step 5: steps 2 through 4 are repeated in a different room
> Step 6: hide the item in an unknown, but easy to locate hiding place without your dog watching
> Step 7: make the hiding places more and more difficult
> Step 8: train negative indication

So far, so good, but our ultimate aim is to have the dog find an arbitrary item belonging to us somewhere outside. Before you read on, try to imagine what the next steps might be. Take your time with this and maybe even write them down. (This exercise will help you with everything you might want to teach your dog as the principles are always the same.)

The following, then, is my suggestion for the next steps.

> Step 9: train with the same item outside; for example in your garden
> Step 10: change location several times
> Step 11: let the dog find a new item at a known place
> Step 12: switch items several times and choose very different ones; for example: wallet, keys, glove, etc

These are our training steps until we have taught our dog to find something we have lost.

Now, there are two more things to consider. Let us assume that your dog has been successful up to step 10. At this point you will have to demonstrate once more what it is that has been taught, and what it is you are now asking the dog to do. This will have a lot to do with the type of object that your dog is searching for. If, for example, you have hidden only items made of cloth until now, you cannot necessarily ask that your dog should now also look for metal objects.

All items have their own scent, so therefore you cannot necessarily expect your dog to find something that someone else has lost. I say "not necessarily" deliberately because, of course, it's quite possible that your dog will do this, as he may have decided "I am searching for everything that smells like my human, no matter what material" in the first instance, or "I am searching for everything that smells of human even if it is not my human" in the second instance. What thoughts he may have and conclusions he may draw we cannot say with certainty, quite apart from the difficulties connected to the fact that dogs perceive their world in very different ways to how we perceive ours.

Always remember that you can only ask your dog to do something if you have taught him how to do it in the first place!

Now, let us assume that your dog is experiencing problems moving from training steps 8 to 9. It might be that he is finding the most complicated hiding places in the house, but does not seem to understand what you want once you go outside. You can resolve this by setting up, say, five more steps between 8 and 9. One possible solution would be to repeat steps 1 through 4 outside: an alternative could be to work your way outside slowly. First, your dog could search in the hallway, then on the stairs, then on the porch, then gradually further and further outside. No matter what it is you want to teach your dog, this way of working will always make your training more effective. You will learn to react to your dog flexibly and to consider adapting any training suggestion, so that you will have an answer each time to help your dog achieve complete understanding of what is required.

Or maybe you've found a different solution altogether?

PRACTICAL APPLICATION

This exercise can also be applied for practical purposes; for example, to teach your dog to look for a specific object. How about your car keys or your mobile phone?

Repeat the first 8 training steps with your car keys: the command could be "Find keys!" Once he has learned to do this, repeat the exercise with your mobile phone, ensuring that your car keys are out of sight so that your dog is not distracted by them.

Once he is able to do each exercise separately, have him search for the mobile phone, but with the car keys visible as well, which will help him to distinguish between the two items. If he should return with the wrong object, don't react but simply let him search again. Also, don't use the word "no" or similar as this will only frustrate him. If he is making too many mistakes, go back a few training steps and start again.

Your dog can also be taught to find a non-specific object, in which case use a command – for example, "Find lost!" – that will make it clear to him that it is not an object he already knows. With the right training, he will also be able to find items belonging to other people, and you and your dog will become a popular team, much in demand, once word spreads!

The foregoing exercise is also very well suited to testing the trailing stamina of your dog. Maybe you are working with rescue dogs, or you do tracking sports and would like to improve your dog's stamina. Let him search for a different number of items more often in order to do this. These are good, fun exercises that you can carry out without too much effort, which will stimulate and interest you both, as well as improve your dog's stamina (and yours, too!).

Please come and visit again!

You and your dog will become popular visitors ...

What's she lost this time?!

WHAT IS MY DOG TELLING ME?

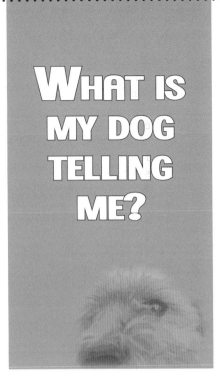

One difficulty with teaching a dog scent work is how to let her know what we want her to do. As detailed in the previous chapter, this can be achieved with small exercise steps and a well planned exercise structure.

Another difficulty is how to determine whether the dog is trying to tell us that she smells something or has found something.

Earlier in the book I mentioned how important it is to observe your dog closely. The best way to achieve this is to use a video camera from time to time so that you are able to watch certain sequences again and again.

When your dog shows you that she has located a scent, or has found something, this is called 'indication.' There are different types of indication, which can be divided into those that a dog uses naturally, and those that a human has trained her to use. We should take a closer look at this subject.

You may have already encountered this problem in the last chapter, if you have a dog that will immediately bring you a found item, or maybe one that will stand in front of the item and wag her tail, or a dog that will find the item but then move away and ignore it. If your dog is in this latter group, you will appreciate how difficult it is to establish whether or not she has actually found something.

In order to circumvent this problem your dog can be trained to use a certain method of indication, although the most reliable method is that which she uses naturally and automatically without the need to think about it. Natural indication will also be the most reliable one in more difficult situations, when your dog may momentarily forget the trained indication method. All of us have been in a situation where an important thing just won't come to mind. We should therefore not judge our dogs for doing this, but rather train them and ourselves to understand what they are telling us.

NATURAL INDICATION
So what is your dog showing you?

Not all dogs indicate a found item as obviously as this!

In this respect every dog is different, and it is not possible to state categorically what your dog will do to indicate naturally, which could be wagging the tail, holding her head higher or lower, or a certain posture she assumes when she smells something. It may be that once she has found something, she might jump around in excitement, or scratch the ground (very clear signals), or may just glance up briefly and assume the job is done.

I can only stress again how useful it is to learn to understand the indications of your dog ('read' your dog) by close observation. In the course of this book, you will be asked to consciously observe and note the details of your dog's expression. What does she look like when she finds a strong scent? What does she look like when following a faint scent? What does she look like when she can't find a scent at all, as described in the example of negative indication in chapter one?

TRAINED INDICATION

In order to make it clearer to you, your dog can be trained to use certain indication types, each of which has its pros and cons. However, it is possible to teach certain indications for certain exercises, in order to use the best possible indication in each case.

Retrieving

In our search for an item, one possible outcome is that your dog brings you the item. Of course, this presupposes that she has learned to take different items, such as car keys, lighters, mobile phones, etc, in her mouth and carry them, if possible, without chewing them.

Lagotto Romagnolos make good nose-work dogs.

A set of keys lost in the high grass. Great if your dog can help you find it!

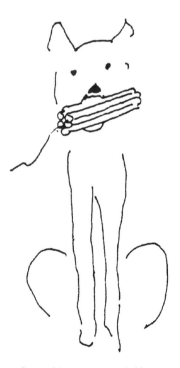

Some objects are not suitable to be retrieved ...

For the purpose of finding lost items this clearly is a useful ability. But if your dog has problems retrieving, there are plenty of other ways for her to track and indicate.

In some situations, such as tracking, it is actually not intended for the dog to take the item in her mouth. Also, in cases where dogs are used to search seriously, for example, to locate drugs or explosives, it would not be very useful for them to pick up their find! Or let us suppose that a lost item belongs to a missing person, and the police want to dust it for fingerprints. Here again, it would not be helpful if the dog's saliva made this impossible.

However, a dog can be trained to retrieve a found object upon the "Find lost!" command, but to indicate by lying down when tracking. We simply have to make it absolutely clear to the dog what we want her to do. In the course of the training process it may be that, from time to time, she uses the 'wrong' indication in a certain exercise. In this instance, just ignore it until she uses the right one by simply pretending not to understand until she tells you in the right way.

Try to avoid using "no," as it is not very helpful and, at best, only tells the dog what she is not supposed to do, which may cause frustration in some cases, as it does not tell her what she *is* supposed to do.

In nature, behaviour patterns that are not useful are used less and less, so to ensure that unwanted behavioural patterns are dropped, do not pay attention to them, whilst ensuring that wanted patterns are rewarded with recognition and praise.

Sitting, standing, lying down

I would like to deal with these indication methods together, as it is generally not important which is used.

No! No! No!

Frustrating for your dog ...

Romeo 'indicates' his quarry by sitting (opposite, top), standing (opposite, bottom), lying down (above) ...

On the track, the most popular indication is lying down, if possible in the direction of the track. In this instance, this is a very useful indication. In the search for a lost item, this indication could also be useful provided the dog can be observed in her work, and is a good alternative if, for example, with a dog that is not so keen on retrieving, you do not want to go through the process of teaching her to do so.

For differentiation between scents, as I cover later, this indication is less useful, for if the dog has twenty items lying in front of her, and simply stands there, or sits or lies down, this does not convey a great deal of information about particular items.

There are many ways to teach a dog a certain type of indication. As examples, I want to present just two of them, both of which can be used to teach indications on a track or when finding things.

The first method is initially taught independently of the track or trail. A prerequisite is that your dog is able to follow the command "Down!" (or "Sit!" or "Stand!," depending on which you want to use).

Place the object on the ground. Once your dog registers that it is there, give the command "Down!" and repeat until she automatically lies down when the object touches the ground (to your dog the object almost becomes the "Down!" command). Up to this point, your dog has remained close to you, but in the next exercise step, she is either a few feet away, or you place the item some distance from her. Upon the command "Down," she should walk to the item and lie down. If this does not work initially, consider introducing some intermediary steps. It may be that the item is too far away, in which case, increase the distance gradually.

In the next step, position the item without your dog watching, but in a place where it can be easily seen. Now, either approach it slowly with your dog, or let her walk on her own (depending on the situation), and simply observe what she does. She should locate the item and lie down without a command from you; only

... and barking!

help if she does something different, and then only once. If your dog has not understood what is required, go back a few steps in the training process.

Next, you should include distraction. Use anything you like for this but ensure you make it exciting for the dog. Most dogs are very excited on a search and sometimes forget what it is they are supposed to do, so deliberately build the excitement, step by step, from the start.

The last stage, before you are really able to use this type of indication on a track or in finding things, is that your dog should generalise this type of indication for all possible items, so repeat the exercise using different objects, and do so before applying this indication in tracking or trailing.

In tracking, there is the additional requirement that the dog lies down in front of the item in the direction she walked, and the best way to achieve this is to only reward her from the front. (Have a second person give the reward, or first walk past your dog before rewarding her. Do this from both left and right sides to keep her from looking around, expecting to find you, and then lying at an angle.) But, please, really take your time to teach this type of indication. I have already mentioned that you should always work on just one aspect at a time. If your dog has not yet mastered indication correctly, and also has to take into account the direction in which she is supposed to lie, this demands too much, and the only thing you create is frustration. As always in training, the most important thing should be to have fun.

The next stage in training this indication should be carried out on a track or a trail. As soon as your dog has understood the task, ie finding things, now is the time to place many more objects on the course, and simply watch what she does. If she walks past the objects, don't worry; this is not a problem. At some point she will stop at one, even if only for a moment, and when she does, make an extra effort to reward her (what, in trainer jargon, is called the 'dog hitting a jackpot,' which could, for example, be a very special treat or a chance to play with her favourite toy). If she wants to go on searching, this is okay, too, as this is also a reward.

In order to acknowledge her stopping next to an item, the clicker is very suitable as a secondary positive amplification. The function of a clicker is explained in other publications (see Appendices). This hesitation will then, gradually, become a definite stop. If your dog has understood this exercise, the many items on the course – which were used only to offer more chances for your dog to succeed and be rewarded – are thinned out and removed.

Barking

Particularly in rescue dog work, barking is used as an indication. The advantage is that this is easy to train and, depending on the surroundings, easy to hear, especially important in situations where the dog can no longer be seen.

The disadvantages, however, are more numerous: although it is easy to train barking, it is relatively difficult to control it with signals. The dog should bark only when she receives the corresponding signal, which may initially be a command or, later, when she locates what or who she is searching for. She should not bark if this signal is not present – and therein lies the problem. Once a dog has discovered that barking can be useful, she will use it more often in other situations.

In order to control barking with signals, it is important not to pay attention to it in any other situation. This is especially difficult, as we humans mainly communicate with spoken words, and therefore are quick to react to a dog's barking. Constant barking – if not controlled with signals – is also very annoying!

Another disadvantage is what the lost person might be having to endure. Imagine you are lying

SMELLORAMA! *Nose games for dogs*

somewhere with a broken leg. A rescue dog finds you, and then stands there barking as loudly as she can until the rescue team arrives. And rescue dogs are usually not small creatures, either!

Barking can also be bad for the dog. Let us assume that the search occurs on a hot day. The dog finds the victim — who is lying in a difficult to access location — and begins to bark. Because of the inaccessibility of the location, it takes rather a long time for the handler to arrive. Under these circumstances barking is a very tiring activity for the dog, which she may need to continue for fifteen minutes or longer. If she then stops barking out of exhaustion, she and the victim may not be found. There are also situations in which barking cannot be heard from a distance.

In America, the most common technique is that the dog, once she has found something, will return to her handler and lead him to the victim. In order to indicate to the handler that something has been found, the rescue dog may use any number of indications, including barking, sitting, jumping, or holding an item in her mouth. In this latter case, the dog will wear a special collar with an item attached to it which she takes in her mouth to let the handler know that she has found the victim.

Barking — not particularly pleasant for the quarry.

WHICH SCENT IS THAT?

The remarkable feats our dogs can perform are never more obvious than in their ability to distinguish scents, identifying one object out of a number which smells different. This may be something that the dog's handler has touched a short time before, and which now lies amongst a number of 'neutral' items, as is the case with an exercise in obedience competitions.

In order to try this exercise you will need a few neutral items which do not yet have a specific scent to them other than their own; quite effective here are beer mats, as long as they are fresh from the box and not previously used (ask your local landlord if he can help with these). The advantage is that they are cheap

As soon as your dog looks at the beer mat – click!

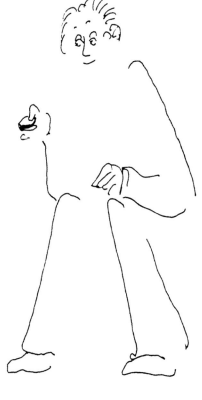

SMELLORAMA! *Nose games for dogs*

Tüddel goes through the beer mats and indicates the right one by lying down in front of it.

Silas learns how to touch and hold a beer mat first before learning to indicate which one smells like his owner ...

... and then bringing it to her.

and you will always have a sufficient supply of fresh ones, with no scent on them, to hand. If you fold a beer mat in the middle it will also be very easy for your dog to pick up, in the event you have decided to teach her retrieving as an indication method. When you are folding and laying out the beer mats, make sure you do not contaminate them with your scent. Disposable latex gloves are useful here as long as you ensure you do not touch them on the outside whilst you are putting them on. Another possibility would be to work with pliers or tweezers, which is easy if the beer mats are already folded.

You might be thinking "Isn't this a bit exaggerated?" Well, not at all. Particularly at the beginning it is important to work with as little scent contamination as possible, even if only to be able to properly communicate to your dog what it is you'd like her to find. We simply cannot just say "Please bring me the item that smells like me," or "... like almond oil," or whatever, as she cannot understand this. For this reason, ensure that the objects bear only one scent.

FIRST EXERCISE: WHERE IS 'MY' BEER MAT?

So, here we go. As always, there are several ways to teach your dog something, and the following exercise covers just one of them. Our first objective is to let your dog find one item, out of a set, which carries the scent in question. In this example we will use retrieving as the method of indication. First, your dog should learn to take a beer mat in her mouth and bring it to you. To achieve this, you might play with the mat in front of your dog and then toss it away. Playful dogs and dogs that love to retrieve should be motivated enough by this to pick up the beer mat and bring it to you. For dogs that do not like to play that much, the clicker can be very helpful here. Click and reward your dog with a treat when she looks at the beer mat, then when she touches it with her nose, then when she takes it in her mouth, and finally when she brings it to you. This is the only stage of training where you can continuously work with one beer mat.

Then use this beer mat for the first scent differentiation exercise. Once your dog has learned well enough to happily bring you this beer mat, deposit (with the pliers if possible) a second, fresh one, approximately 5 feet away from the first one and from your dog. Praise your dog extensively if she brings you the original beer mat; this is made easier for her by the greater distance to the second beer mat. If she brings the wrong one, do not pay any attention to this, but simply replace the mat with a new one and repeat the exercise. Do not reprimand her if she brings you the wrong one; she is allowed to make mistakes as this is the only way for her to learn what you really want. A 'wrong' signal, which lets her know that a certain behaviour did not lead to success would be very useful for this exercise, but it should not be punishment; nor a loud, shouted "No!" but plain, neutral information. A well-trained 'wrong' signal, used in conjunction with the clicker to show your dog which is the right way, seems to be an effective way to communicate.

It's important that the 'wrong' signal is not given too often. The level of difficulty is right if you are able to give the praising click in more than 70 per cent of instances: if the 'wrong' signal has to be given in more than 30 per cent of cases, the exercise is too difficult, which means you should go back a few training steps.

Slowly but steadily the two different beer mats are placed closer together, until they are only a few inches apart. Once your dog is able to bring you the right beer mat in nine out of ten cases, you can add a third one. Increase the number of beer mats one by one to as many as you like. In the end, your dog should be able to locate the right one from an entire stack of beer mats.

Up until this point your dog has searched for its own, specific training beer mat, which was used to give her an idea of the rules of this game. Now comes the actual exercise ...

In order to do this you first have to make a decision. You can turn your dog into a specialist to find one specific scent, which she will then be able to locate under any and all circumstances, or you can decide to have her search for different scents you provide. It is important that you clearly define what your dog is to do. Only then can you lead her towards the task. Also, you should always question whether the method you are using is the right way to teach her to do what it is you want.

SECOND EXERCISE: WHICH BEER MAT DID I HOLD?

For this exercise you will need four beer mats, or four other identical items. Lay out two mats, if possible using pliers or wearing latex gloves, without your dog watching. Hold the other two in your hands and thoroughly rub them a few times (treat these two items as equally as possible). Place one of them next to the two neutral ones; the other will become the scent pattern for your dog.

Show this to your dog, and let her take in the scent. Ask her to find the other item that bears your scent and bring it to you, or indicate it in some way. As this item has your scent, it's okay to hold it without wearing gloves. Later, when you are teaching other scents, the pattern item should not be contaminated with your scent until your dog has understood what is expected.

You can work without a pattern, of course, but using one has the advantage of allowing you to teach your dog a wide range of exercises.

Once your dog has learned to indicate the one beer mat that has your scent, you can refine this exercise, initially by replacing the beer mats with other items which, at first, have to be completely new and should not be from your household. Later, used items may be introduced as well, with the dog merely indicating the one that you most recently held in your hand.

You may want to expand this exercise to include items that other people have held in their hands. Again, begin with the beer mats. Take two neutral ones and two that a friend has held – initially, for quite a while – in their hands. As before, one of these 'contaminated' beer mats is used as the pattern and the other is placed next to the neutral ones. Take great care not to contaminate the beer mat with your own scent; work with pliers or ask the other person to place the beer mat that is to be found.

Once your dog has understood this exercise, pick anything that carries the scent of the other person to use as a pattern – which could be the person themself!

You could then repeat this exercise with everyone who comes to visit you, slowly, and with more and more different items.

Now you can ask two people to touch items and give your dog the task of differentiating between the two. There are no limits to the variations of this exercise. For your dog this is fun, and you can surprise and impress many people with your dog's abilities.

THIRD EXERCISE: WHICH BEER MAT SMELLS OF MILK?

Apart from the scents of different people you can also have your dog sniff out many other smells, and it is interesting to dilute the scent more and more to see how faint it can be and still be detected by your dog.

Let us use our pattern beer mats again. By now your dog is sufficiently acquainted with this exercise and you can confidently lay out four, five or six mats. In this exercise the neutral beer mats are 'treated' also: take a bowl of water and dip the beer mats in, holding them with your pliers. Let them drip off and lay them out.

To the bowl of water, add roughly one quarter of its volume of milk. Dip in two more beer mats, let them drip off as well, put one of them next to the neutral ones and keep the other with you. Then summon your dog, let her smell the pattern mat and have her search the laid out beer mats. If she indicates the wrong one, don't say "No!" or anything else, just ignore it. If she should return with the right one, praise her as if she had performed a miracle. Repeat the exercise until your dog indicates the correct beer mat in 90 per cent of cases. You can continue to use the neutral items unless your dog has touched them. If your dog indicates without retrieving, you can also reuse the milky beer mats. Otherwise, you will require new ones.

Once your dog has understood the task "find the milky beer mat," dilute the milky water more and more. If, for the previous exercise, you added one quarter of the volume (which equated to a pint of milk), now use half a pint.

Repeat the exercise as described above. Once your dog is able to bring you the correct beer mat in 90 per cent of cases, you can dilute the mix further. If she brings you the right beer mat in 60 per cent of cases, go back a step. Remember that a dog will learn best if she succeeds.

How much can you dilute the milk water with the dog still being able to find the right, contaminated beer mat? You may be surprised ...

Again, consider what it is that you want. With this method you can turn your dog into a specialist for

A small amount of milk is added to the water ...

... and the beer mat submerged in the solution.

a specific substance, which she will be able to find under all circumstances. This could, for example, be milk. But what happens if the milk has been boiled? Will your dog recognise this? You could train this as a distinguishing feature, or train her to indicate milk in any condition, which could be useful for people with allergies. In this case, your dog should be trained to identify milk in other mixtures, for example in pudding, ice cream, sauce, etc. A good way to present these mixtures is in jars that have holes in their lids. However, remember that working with foodstuffs requires a very high training standard. You must be certain that your dog is actually indicating the milk, and not dancing a jig simply because there is something tasty in the jar!

FOLLOWING TRAILS

This chapter deals with the subject of trailing. Not tracking, which is something completely different, and which I do not cover in this book for two reasons: one, there is already sufficient literature about it on the market, and two, I believe that tracking does not challenge dogs sufficiently and they become bored. And I have also found it very boring to mark out a track and position treats in the footprints!

A long time ago I was able to witness how my very young dog (I don't believe that he was any older than 12 weeks) followed the scent of a cat, which I had earlier seen walk over the grass. Directly behind a molehill the cat changed direction at a right angle, walked thirty yards or so in a straight line, turned left and jumped over a wall. When the pup came into the garden he followed the cat's trail precisely and retraced the angle exactly. He finally sniffed the wall, shortly before turning away to do other things.

In that moment the penny dropped: the cat had not *stamped* out a track, it had walked very lightly, and at an angle that had never been taught to the dog, who just knew how to do it. And this is why I believe that dogs are extremely under-challenged when it comes to tracking, and they are asked to repeat, time and time again, actions which clearly they have been born knowing how to do. We return to the earlier example of writing lines. Very boring!

I also believe that the only reason dogs sometimes have problems with angles is that they are taught initially — and for a long time — that tracks are straight. When I train dogs, angles are used right from the start and the dogs have no problem with them.

Searching games are suitable — and great fun! — even for pups.

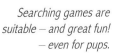

37

SMELLORAMA! Nose games for dogs

Another aspect I am unhappy about in tracking is how the dog is trained to seek out particular ground disturbance, and follow the footsteps as precisely as possible. Experiments have been carried out whereby a person has laid a track up to a point, and then has been lifted off the track by a crane. A wheel — of the same weight as the person, and with the same shoes attached to it at pacing distances corresponding to those of the person — has taken over the track laying, which the dogs followed without noticing any difference ...

Another experiment had two V-shaped tracks laid out by two different people, meeting at a single point. The dogs followed one track up to the point where the two tracks met, and then switched to the other track at the V-point, which meant that they were now tracking someone else.

These experiments have demonstrated to me how little tracking has to do with the nature of dogs.

Let us return to laying out trails, so that you can see for yourself how different this is.

LAYING TRAILS

Before we begin the practical, a few dry runs without your dog are necessary. Particularly in the early stages of training it is extremely important that you know the exact course of the trail that you, or someone else, has laid out, and should have memorised this before beginning to work with your dog. When you are working with your dog, you must be able to concentrate on him and not whether you can remember where the trail is supposed to lead.

To start with, take a writing pad outside into the field with you so that you can sketch out the trail as precisely as possible. The following is a description of a method of doing this, which works fine for us, but does not mean that you can't come up with a better one. The following criteria are important:
The trail should be defined clearly, so that it could still be followed a few days later.
The signs used should be concise, but clear enough for someone else to read them.

Define a starting point and a direction indicator (this could be a certain marking, or something in the field). Be careful with things such as molehills, though, as the mole may dig additional hills the following day, and you won't be able to remember which is the correct one.

In order to indicate the direction of travel, use a specific landmark in the distance, towards which you will move. If you want to include an angle, this should be clearly defined as well. When moving, the landmarks will be perceived differently to when you stand still, appearing to get closer together, maybe overlap at some point and then separate again. The position at which two landmarks overlap can be used as an angle marker (see the photographs on page 49). The chosen landmarks here are the furthest left of the four fence posts and the oak. The closer you get, the closer together they get, until they appear to be in line. This spot will be the position of your angle.

From here, pick a new landmark in the distance to define your new direction; this completes the exact definition of your angle. When laying out your trails, eventually, you will not need to write this down, although I recommend doing so as a training diary.

In this, also note down the time you laid out the trail, the weather, the time your dog worked on the trail, again the weather, wind direction, results and difficulties experienced. In this way you can always assess how well training is going.

Another method is to mark the way. One of the participants in our course uses red plastic clothes pegs, which are perfectly suitable, but you should not simply place a peg at each angle you include in your course, as this will very quickly become too easy for your dog. Spread the pegs — seemingly at random — around the course (as far as you can reach without leaving the trail). This will give you additional aids to better find your trail; for example, you might walk at a right angle to the left, three paces after the fourth marker, until the third marker from there, etc.

Markings along the trail should be clearly visible to the human, but barely discernible to your dog.

One advantage of working with these markers is that you can leave yourself hints. A disadvantage is that the markers will have to be collected up again once you have finished. For longer trails we also like to use clothes pegs with ribbons as markers (see page 39). These can be easily attached to branches to mark the way, as in a treasure hunt. If you work with coloured clothes pegs, a blue one could mean "this is the right way," and a red one "go right after this," for example, or whatever you choose to assign to it. Ask your friends to walk a trail marked in this way to see which parts are unclear.

LEASH TRAINING FOR PEOPLE

Before you start working with your dog, I recommend one more dry run. I will describe the trailing process using the long leash, which can be used to give a clear signal to your dog. I also train rescue dogs for area scanning without a leash, but, once the dogs are on a leash, they understand that they are not supposed

Lisa is preparing Darja for the search.

Dry runs with the long leash are important. First, tie the leash to a fence, and then use a human helper in place of a dog.

to scan for human scent with their noses high in the air, but follow just one scent trail. If this differentiation is clear enough (which includes different commands, as well as an adapted training set-up), then a dog can certainly learn to distinguish between searching methods. Of course, this also depends on the dog, the clear commands of the dog handler, and the time available for training. Some trainers advocate starting with detailed training, ie: tracking or following scent trails, and only begin scanning areas later; others the exact opposite. I believe each trainer should develop a feeling for each dog and dog handler he is dealing with, to determine the right technique for each team. Trainers should also be flexible enough to try something different once in a while, as long as it concurs with the rules of learning, in order to master as many techniques as possible.

A further advantage of the long leash is that dogs with a tendency to hunt will also master this exercise well, without fear that they might run away. I use following scent trails specifically as part of a therapy for dogs that tend to hunt, as this represents a very good alternative for the dog. Once dogs such as these are on the trail, and after some training, they forget their preference for hunting.

The long leash also allows the dog's actions to be read, and thus to recognise what it is the dog is signalling. For this reason, the leash should always be kept fairly tight. Just as the reins of a bridle are used to establish a direct connection to the horse's mouth, the leash can be used to build a subtle connection to the dog. Now if the dog hesitates – for whatever reason – this is immediately registered through the leash, which has become our 'direct line' to our dog.

However, this presupposes sensitive usage of the leash, which should always be at the same tension, even if the dog changes direction or speed.

This brings us to the dry run I mentioned. Attach the leash to a fixed spot, such as a fence, and first practise shortening and lengthening the leash, keeping the tension the same. You will quickly appreciate that this is not at all easy! As the leash is tied to one spot, you will need to walk forwards and backwards to do this; to lengthen the leash, just let it slide through your hands, but wear gloves when doing so to protect your hands (which I recommend whenever working with a leash). An alternative is to let out small lengths a little at a time. See which is easier for you and how you are best able to keep the tension constant. Mark a spot, shortly before the end of the leash, for example with a knot. This will let you know without looking that you have no more leash to play out, or you might otherwise lose the leash altogether.

When shortening the leash, you will have to do this bit by bit, and, depending on how wide apart you move your hands, you can vary the speed. Also practise taking up the leash quickly, which will be necessary whenever your dog stops abruptly. Once you are able to keep the tension relatively equal with the leash tied to a fixed spot, use a person as a substitute dog and practise again. Your helper should hold the line and give you feedback about how it feels while you walk together. Is the tension equal or are there variations? After a while, your 'dog' should try and change speed abruptly to challenge you more and more.

This exercise is especially important for sensitive dogs, as well as those that have been trained to react to a pull on the leash. Dogs which have always been led on a loose leash and do not have experience of the leash being pulled also need this preparation, as, with a single pull, it should be possible to lead your dog away from the trail, or from working altogether. For this reason I place much importance on practising working with a leash beforehand.

It may occur to some readers that a retractable leash would be just the thing for this type of work; after all, it will retract and extend by itself and save you the effort of practising this. With the help of your human 'dog,' use both types of leash at the same time, and I think you will find that the retractable leash provides much less 'feeling' and connection to your dog.

Another feature that makes the retractable leash unusable for our needs will become apparent in the following exercise.

Unlike as with tracking, when a dog follows a trail he does not need to exactly trace the footsteps of the person that left it, but rather the scent trail, which may actually lie several feet to the side of the walked trail. Now if, say, the trail is on a forest path, it is very possible that your dog will walk parallel to the path, but behind the first row of trees, in which case you could either walk behind him (which might be awkward), or you could release the leash for a moment and pick it up again after the obstacle. (This should also be practised with your two-legged 'dog.')

The next important topic is leash rolling up. Most people roll up long leashes over their hand and elbow, as in skeining wool. The result is an arrangement of parallel loops, which can easily become entangled when released. A good way to roll up the leash is that which is often used for knitting wool: a plain, tight, round ball. This is also possible with a long leash and means it cannot become tangled and will unroll easily, making

SMELLORAMA! Nose games for dogs

Make sure that you give out leash without knots in it.

Roll up the leash as you would a ball of wool to prevent it from becoming tangled.

giving out more leash very simple. Note, though, that you cannot do this with a wet leash, as it will not have a chance to dry. Decide which method suits you best, but ensure that the leash is not knotted in any way as your dog begins its search.

Regarding the leash itself; many different lengths, diameters and materials are available. I recommend you start with a 3 metre leash as this will be easier to control. Later on, your dog can work at a greater distance.

The diameter of the leash should correspond to the size of your dog. Generally, a thicker leash will sit better in your hand, but will also mean that the leash is heavier, which can represent an unnecessary burden for him. For this reason, the leash diameter should not exceed 5-6mm for a medium-sized dog (border collie, cocker spaniel, etc). For larger dogs the leash can be up to 8mm in diameter. These sizings apply to synthetic leashes, which are usually round. For leather leashes, sizing applies to their width.

The thickness of the leash should be in proportion to the size of your dog.

Shall we swop leads?

This brings us to the question of material. Synthetic leashes are very easy to clean; a disadvantage is that they may injure your skin, which is why wearing gloves is recommended. There are vast quality differences with leather leashes. Really good, soft leather leash lie very well in your hand, even in wet weather, but they are not cheap. To begin with, use a homemade leash – made out of a piece of string with a snap-link at the end – to work with your dog to gauge whether you both enjoy trailing. If you do, think then about buying an expensive leash.

TRAILING WITHOUT A LEASH

Of course, you can also train your dog to follow trails without a leash, but, in order to do so, he has to learn to work at the desired distance. If the leash is not needed as a signal to your dog to distinguish following a scent trail from a different type of search, this may – depending on the dog – be an alternative which is especially useful in the forest, as long as the dog has no tendency to hunt. However, remember that you will be not have the 'direct line' to your dog, through which a lot information is exchanged.

LEASH TRAINING FOR YOUR DOG

After you have learned how to use the long leash, you should begin to slowly acquaint your dog with it. At your dog's end, what is missing is the searching harness. When choosing the harness, first ensure that it fits correctly. Some harnesses can be adjusted around the stomach only; if the neck part fits well, you are

SMELLORAMA! Nose games for dogs

Your dog should not want to use the opportunity of being off-lead to run away from you!

Oh, she's just doing a spot of tracking ...

lucky. Generally, a better choice is a harness that can be adjusted around the stomach and around the neck.

It should not rub on the skin. One cause of this can be buckles that lie directly on the fur; on a good harness, the buckles are lined underneath to prevent this.

The material should be nice and soft or padded. Wearing the harness must be comfortable for your dog to ensure he enjoys the work and is not upset by a bothersome harness that does not fit well.

Check that the harness will not hinder your dog in his searching work: he should be able to lower his head without the breast belt cutting into his neck. If you press on your own breast bone, you can do it fairly strongly without it becoming very uncomfortable, but if you move a few centimetres further up, it becomes very uncomfortable the harder you press. For this reason, nothing should be pressing into your dog's neck, even when his nose is touching the ground.

Once you have found a good harness, give your dog plenty of opportunity to get used to it. Most dogs have no problem with them, but it does, obviously, feel somewhat different from what he has been used to. So let him wear the harness for a while, until he no longer pays it any attention, after which, it should only ever be worn for a search. In this way the harness becomes an important signal for your dog and tells him what is expected.

If your dog usually wears a harness anyway, the long leash can be attached to it directly, and this will become an indicator to tell him that it is time to search.

THE BAG

One way to present a scent to your dog that you wish him to trail is to place an item with the scent on it in a plastic bag (if possible with a zip-lock). When you are ready to begin, the dog is supposed to put his nose inside the bag to take in the scent, and to find the trail that contains it.

Using a bag means that the scent is preserved within it, and the bag may be touched by different people without the scent being affected. This also means that a scent pattern can be transported. When working with your own scent this is not important – in that case you can simply put an item in your pocket. But as soon as you begin working with someone else's scent it is important to present the dog with an unaltered

When choosing the searching harness, make sure that it does not press on the dog's throat when she has her nose to the ground. Here are two different models of harness.

Now that Immie's into tracking in such a big way, we're no longer of interest to her!

45

You will be able to tell straight away whether or not your dog is happy to put his nose into the bag.

No practise necessary in this case!

Never force the bag over your dog's nose.

initial pattern. Also, a bag can be used to store very small amounts of material with a scent, such as the scent on a ring, which I will come to later.

Your dog will have to learn to put his nose into the bag, and you should prepare for and practise this right from the start, to avoid scaring or worrying your dog by attempting to put a bag over his nose on the first search you undertake.

Take a bag, put two or three treats inside and offer this to your dog. How does he react? Some dogs will quickly and without fuss put their muzzles into the bag and retrieve the treats; for these, no more practise is required! Many others, though, are reluctant and suspicious until they begin to connect the bag with something

Even something as small as a ring in a plastic bag can provide enough scent for your dog to track and find the ring's wearer.

pleasant, such as a treat or a toy. Practise for a few days, until your dog will put his nose into the bag willingly and without hesitation.

WORKING WITH YOUR OWN TRAIL

We have worked through all of the preliminary exercises, so now let us begin. You may want to fill a backpack with all of the things you will need for this search; this will also let your dog know what is about to happen. The following is a list of all the things you should remember to pack:

SMELLORAMA! Nose games for dogs

Julie picks up the scent from the bag.

Searching harness
Long leash
Water, which you should offer your dog before each search, and during long searches
Writing pad
Pencils: these will write in any weather; ballpoint pens might fail in wet weather
Various items with the scent to be indicated, such as a glove, a sock, a piece of cloth, a piece of leather, a cap, etc, all with your scent
Possibly plastic bags with zip-locks
Tools to mark the trail, such as clothes pegs or tent pegs
Rewards for your dog (toys or treats)

We have already dealt with most of the things that are necessary to lay out the trail, so I will assume that you have practised laying out a trail and that re-discovering it is not a problem for you. We will begin with very simple trails anyway, and you will become more and more used to laying them.

With the first trail your dog should be watching. Lay it out in a field and mark the starting point; this could be with one of the items, which your dog can use to pick up the scent later on, but doesn't have to be. It is only important that you know where the trail begins. Then walk twenty to thirty paces towards a landmark in the distance. After about 15 paces begin to look for a way to mark your angle. At a point where two landmarks at different distances appear to overlap, walk toward the right of them at roughly a right angle: how roughly depends on the position of your new target landmark; if there's nothing exactly at a right angle, the angle can be more acute or obtuse.

While you are walking, pretend to put down the treats or the toy that your dog knows from the "Find!" exercise. However, only actually do this at the end of your trail — a further 20 or so paces — and without your dog seeing you do so.

Your dog should recognise your actions from the exercises you've done together previously. However, now, he has the additional assistance of your scent, which he needs only to follow. To ensure this happens, initially, the wind should be at your back (see drawing on page 50), so that he does not smell the target right away and walk straight towards it.

At the end of the trail take some especially long steps and walk back in a wide arc; under no circumstances should you walk back along the set trail.

The way the exercise is set up now is very simple for your dog, as long as he has first learned to find items in the house. The one learning step that is new to him in this context is the bag, although you will have practised with this and familiarised him with what he must do with it. In order for this to work you should have in your bag a replica of the item that you hid, ie: the same toy, or the same treats.

Using different landmarks at a distance you can define a certain location where you can include an angle in the trail.

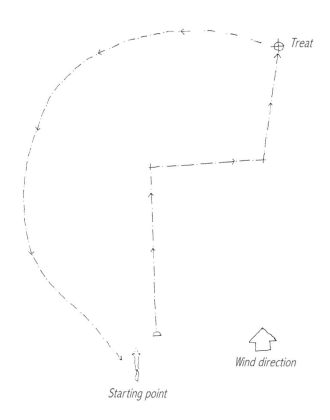

Treat

Wind direction

Starting point

You should have held both toys or treats in your hands for the same amount of time, so that they smell similar to you. After a while your dog should understand that what the item looks like is not important, but that what it smells of is. Later on, the items can be different, but at the beginning we want to make it nice and simple for him.

Now lead your dog to within a few feet of the start of the trail, put on his searching harness and attach the long leash. Lay out the leash, checking for knots or tangles. Also ensure that no one stands on the leash. Take the bag, open it, and let your dog sniff the item inside (a single whiff is sufficient).

Another method is to position the first scented item at the start of the trail and let your dog pick up the scent there. This is useful for him to learn and we will build this into the exercise later, as it is a way to make the exercise more interesting, and it will also let you work more flexibly later in other applications.

Use just one of the methods initially, though, until you are certain about the process of the exercise. Then you can consider including variations.

Should your dog not show any interest in the item at the start of the trail, the plastic bag will allow you to help him as it will more-or-less 'force' him to take in the scent. Please do not misunderstand me here, though; do not on any account push the plastic bag over your dog's nose by force! The preliminary exercises that you did before beginning the trail will have shown your dog that the plastic bag is something great, and he should put his nose inside freely and willingly, whereupon he will automatically inhale the scent, simply by breathing in.

Here, Sascha is picking up the scent his owner has laid out.

Find it!
Find it!
Find it!

Find what?!

While your dog has his nose in the bag, give the command "Find!" (give it only at that moment, not later). This will tell him to find something with the scent that is in his nose right now. If you repeat the command more often later, you cannot be sure what scent the dog is smelling at that moment; it could be the trail of another dog, or something else. If he hears your "Find!" command in that moment, you will distract him from his original scent trail. This is the most difficult aspect of working with scents; we cannot smell what the dog does.

Because of the preliminary exercises in the house, your dog should know already what we are expecting, even without the bag. However, for now we will continue to use the bag with the scent item at the start of the search, to ensure that he learns the process, and is not confused later, when we work with foreign scents.

If your dog begins walking well, following the scent on the trail, give him more leash. If he goes too fast,

simply ask him to slow. This is important at the beginning, until you both are used to exercise on a trail. Remember to wear gloves. Let your dog do his work without interfering. If he misses the angle, let him find the way back to the trail by himself. Try not to help — not even unconsciously, via your body movement, otherwise your dog may come to believe that you have the superior nose, and rely on you when in doubt.

Use "Where is it?" to encourage him to continue searching, and try and avoid a second "Find!" command. Be concise and limited in everything you say. Experience has shown that talking distracts dogs much more than it helps them. One "Find!" at the start and one or two instances of "Where is it?" in between should be all you need to say during the search.

Most dogs will begin to move in circles if they lose a trail, which is quite normal, as this technique allows them to find their way back to the scent and continue trailing it. The leash should be long enough to accommodate this, and this is where your preliminary exercise with the two-legged dog can help you as you should have learnt how to keep the leash under steady tension, even if the dog stops abruptly or changes direction.

Once your dog has found the object at the end of the trail, give him much praise, and the treats or toy he has found. Much more important, though, is that you let him know how great you think he is and really express your joy! Some people have problems doing this, so it is worth practising. You could even have someone video you while you are praising your dog, so that afterwards you can see it from your dog's point of view, and consider whether what you see would impress you if you were him. Often it appears very boring and low-key!

WHAT TO DO IF YOUR DOG DOES NOT SEARCH?

Is he not interested at all, or just too distracted? If he has recently been fed, it could be that the treats are not of interest as he is full up. Do your search before he is fed.

Did he properly understand the task when you carried it out in the house? Is he aware that he is supposed to search? Of course, it's possible to search for trails outside even if you haven't done the preliminary exercise in the house. But in this case it is important that you motivate your dog well, and if you can't, go through the searching games in the house before searching scent trails outside.

I am convinced that successfully sniffing out a trail is a reward in itself, and once your dog has understood the concept, he will follow the trail of his own volition.

After the first successfully followed trail comes the next, which should, in principle, be similar, except for the fact that now the angle should go in the opposite direction. And we can set up more and more new challenges for our dog and make the search more and more exciting. Three aspects should be changed over time: the length of the trail, the number of angles, and the ground type.

Practise — at least initially — two to three times per week, and for two to three hours each time. The number of scent trails that you can get through, of course, depends on the searching capabilities of your dog. It has been observed that, initially, shorter trails are preferred, as they are better able to teach your dog the underlying principle. This means that he receives the reward more often and we are better able to increase motivation. Later on, it is no longer necessary to exercise so frequently. At that point your dog will still know what to do, even after a break of, say, three weeks. But at the beginning of training such a long break would mean you would have to start all over again, which would be frustrating for you and your dog.

Feel free to increase the trail distances to 40-60 paces, and by another 20 paces with each new search. Note down the length of each trail in your training diary, so that you always know the state of your progress.

Regarding angles, ensure that you regularly change the order and/or the direction, or try two angles in the same direction one after the other. Be flexible.

Another thing to vary is the length of the trail legs; don't always take a turn after 20 paces, but try doing so after 5 or 40 paces, for example.

Endeavour to include different ground types in the exercise early on, so that your dog does not become used to a specific underlying scent, as the ground obviously has a scent of its own. See for yourself! Smell grass in a meadow, a freshly ploughed acre, or the tarmac! These strong, underlying ground scents must be completely ignored by the dog, who should concentrate on the human trail only.

Note down the exact course of the trails that you follow, the different ground surfaces, the weather, the wind direction and any other peculiarities. Then, should your dog ever experience a problem in any situation, this will help you determine why.

Next, she'll turn left, then straight on, then right, then ...

MORE TRAILING CHALLENGES

INDICATING OBJECTS

Having your dog locate objects during a search can make an entertaining change from simply following a trail. You might begin with a shorter trail that you know your dog is familiar with. The objects you use must bear the same scent as the one that you give your dog to smell at the start of the search.

There are various ways to explain to your dog what it is you want her to do, as described in chapter 2. Should your dog walk past the object, don't scold her, and don't pull on the leash either. Simply walk to the object and say something like: "Look what I found here! Did you overlook this?" She will not understand your words, but your tone should be enough to tell her that you feel sorry she has missed this opportunity. Any dog with the least shred of ambition will not want this to happen very often, and will try harder the next time.

Anyone who places too great an importance on object indication would be better off doing traditional tracking, training the dog to seek out disturbance to the ground, because, with scent trailing, depending on wind and type of ground, it may be that the scent is not present over the entire trail, in which case it will be difficult or even impossible for a dog to indicate objects that are too far from where she is searching.

WORKING WITH A FOREIGN TRAIL

Everything concerned so far with searching for scents can be applied to training your dog to search for a foreign scent also, but, in order to do this, you will need a helper. It would be ideal if this was someone who trains their dog to search for trails as well, and therefore knows what is important here, and you could lay out trails for each other. Of course, you can teach someone to be a helper, initially being nearby when they lay a trail, but not walking alongside. You should also agree on a common system to define direction changes, and I recommend that your helper lays the trail according to your system.

Then you will need objects that have your helper's scent, and this will be easiest to achieve if you use objects belonging to that person, and not just things he or she has briefly held in their hand. As before, start with simple trails and slowly increase the degree of difficulty.

What does your dog do and how does she act whilst following the new scent? Is she as motivated as when following your scent trails? In this respect, for the first time it may be advantageous for your helper to be someone that your dog knows well, but you should swop and change your helpers from then on.

By now you should be able to read your dog well enough to know where she is leading you on the search. You may want to ask your helper to deposit an object just after each angle, which will confirm that you

The quarry rewards the dog with tasty treats for finding her!

are on the right trail. You should, however, not begin doing this until your dog is very secure in the search and finds the target nine times out of ten. If this is not yet the case, it is important that *you* know the trail well, so that you can either help your dog by giving her another whiff of the scent pattern, or by aborting the search and finding out why it went wrong. In the latter instance, you should lay out another, short and simple trail in order to finish the day with your dog being successful.

Experiment further with trail length and with various ground surfaces. Later on, you might ask a passing jogger to give you an item with his scent on it. This could be a fresh paper tissue, used to wipe his brow, and which you can put into your zip-locked plastic bag. He could do the same with a second tissue and drop it about two miles down the road (which you can then pick up). This is one way to relatively easily gain access to someone else's trail, although don't try this until you and your dog are sufficiently confident about following trails.

MISGUIDANCE

Misguidance is what we call other trails that cross the trail we are following, and which your dog should not be distracted by. If you have already included existing paths in your searches, you may have practised misguidance without realising it, as you can't know what other trails are also present on the path. If you really build up your trail practice step-by-step, this should not be a big problem anyway.

In order to increase your dog's confidence, and to better understand her abilities, you should deliberately include misguidance in the search. In this respect, it could again be advantageous if you know someone who trains their dog to follow trails, as you could lay trails that can cross at some point (see drawing opposite). The more acute the crossover angle, the more 'enticing' the misguidance is.

Let each dog follow their own trail. Are they misguided? Do they even hesitate at the spot where the two trails intersect? Do the dogs maybe follow the misguidance for a bit, only to return to search for the right trails again? Observe your dogs carefully: you will learn a lot.

Once this method works well you could again lay out trails that overlap at some point and let your dogs follow each other's trail. Do they more easily become misguided, and choose to follow a more familiar scent? Do not forget to lavishly praise your dog if she remains on the right trail, as this would be a terrific achievement.

To increase the difficulty, you could lay trails that cross over several times, at various angles. Begin the trails at the same point — possibly overlapping — separate later and then cross over again: there are no limits to what can be done — let your imagination run free! This type of training, where dogs work together, can be very enjoyable. And if the dogs have reached this level of experience, you will have reason to admire their olfactory abilities time and time again.

You could also try and lay out, or have laid out, a trail that crosses a deer pass. Will your dog stay true to the trail, do you think? If yes, this is definitely worth a reward. If not, you should repeat the beginner stages, as this is an advanced exercise.

OLD TRAILS

Until now we have had our dogs search for relatively fresh trails. The scent of a trail changes with age. Imagine a person dragging a tunnel of scent behind him: once he stops, the scent will spread out in all directions, initially in a ball shape. Once the person moves again, another 'scent tunnel' is created.

The olfactory particles that comprise the tunnel sink to the ground relatively quickly, and, after a while, all that's left of the scent tunnel is a trail on the ground. This scent trail is then subject to various weather phenomena. In warm weather the trail can again rise into the air. You may already have noticed that, in warm weather, your dog holds her nose higher than in cooler weather, and this is especially so with older trails.

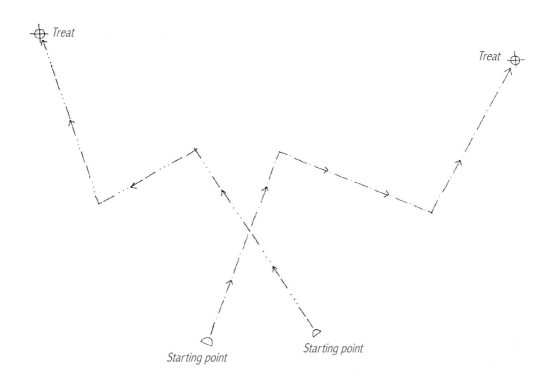

Intense sunshine essentially burns the olfactory particles, making it difficult for your dog to find the right direction from what remains. This is particularly true on tarmac, as here the olfactory particles are exposed to sunshine completely unprotected. In grass they are better preserved, and moist weather will also preserve them, usually making it much easier for dogs to find trails. It is even possible that an older trail which has been exposed to intense sunlight could become clearer again due to light rain or morning dew.

A possible explanation of why this happens is the activation of bacteria. I have previously described how each dead skin cell that is shed by our body is infested with bacteria. If the weather is too hot and dry, the bacteria will shut down their metabolic activities, but they are able to restart them if it becomes more humid. In that case, more gases are created, which the dog can smell.

These changes to the trails affect the scent image, of course. Depending on the age of the trail, it may look very different, which will make it very difficult for your dog to follow. This is the challenge of an older trail, and various methods and opinions exist about how best to tackle these. Some trainers work with at least 4 hour old trails from the start, and once the dog has mastered these, younger trails can be used. This is a very good way to proceed if you have a dog that is very well motivated to search, and which does not need to be shown how you walked down the trail, pretending to place items along it. After this time period the trail has 'settled' and all olfactory particles have reached the ground, where the trail is best defined.

Most people begin with young trails, which are left lying for longer and longer later on, until the dog is asked to follow it. You may have to work in 5 minute intervals in order to do this successfully: once the first 20 minute trail is solved, you can increase trail age by five minutes each time. At the start you could also experiment with longer intervals of time. If your dog has problems with these, simply return to the younger trail age and work towards older trails in even smaller intervals. How old can a trail be that a dog is still able to follow? Well, there have been reports of a dog that was able to follow a week-old trail, but, of course, it very much depends on weather conditions and the dog's training. Under these extreme conditions, breed could also play a role as the genetic traits the dogs have been born with are evident here. But even if you don't have a bloodhound, you can attempt an exercise like this one; even atypical breeds can achieve surprising things if they are trained well, step-by-step. Ultimately, it should really be the enjoyment that person and dog experiences that is the most important consideration.

FINDING PEOPLE

The principle of area scanning — used to train rescue dogs — is that a dog will scan an area for human scent

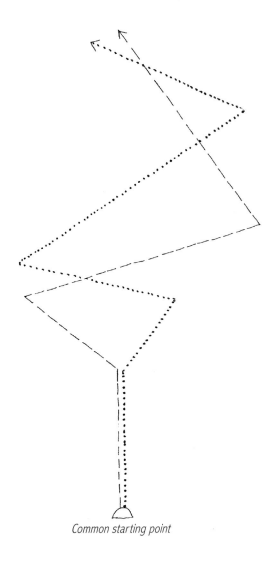

Common starting point

Young Ole is incited by his quarry to search for her.

Minnie has found her quarry hiding in the long grass.

by raising her nose in the air. With the right training, a dog can indicate every person present in the given area. She can also follow the scent of a specific person: recently, the term 'mantrailing' has been used to describe this type of search. In contrast to area scanning, the dog does not indicate just anybody in an area but follows the scent of a specific person, clearly defined with a pattern smell.

In comparison to how we have trained before with your dog, the only difference now is that, rather than a toy or treats waiting for her at the end of the trail, there's a person with these things. Ask your helper to hide at the end of the trail when setting up the search, with the reward. When your dog reaches the end of the trail, she should be well rewarded by both helper and handler. A well socialised dog that is not afraid of people should not have any problems with this.

Another way to make a search for a human more interesting for your dog is to let her see how her quarry runs away to hide: this is also a good way to introduce trailing to dogs which are difficult to persuade with toys or treats.

For the trail, initially, you should use a relatively straight forest path. Begin by asking your helper to hold your dog, who should already be wearing the harness with the long leash. Get your dog's attention with a treat or a toy, or even just your voice, and then run away. After 100-150 metres, hide behind a tree or a bush, no more than a metre or two from the path. Mark the spot with a clothes-peg at eye level where you leave the path, which will make it easier for the handler.

Until now your dog has been able to see what you are doing, but this won't stop her from using her nose on the search. Although she knows that you disappeared somewhere 'over there,' she will not be able to remember the exact spot, because dogs do not have very strong visual thinking abilities.

Now she is given the plastic bag with your scent in it and is sent off with the command "Find!" Exactly as described in finding trails, the command is given only once at this point, because that is the only moment at which we can be absolutely sure that the scent in the dog's nose is the one we want her to search for. Play out the leash to allow her more range and let her search. In this case, her relationship with the handler is useful for motivation. This exercise can actually be attempted with pups, as soon as they have forged a connection to their owner/handler.

As she searches, often it may appear that she is just walking without using her nose, but I believe that a dog's nose works as automatically as do our eyes: we don't need to concentrate especially to see something, we just see it.

It is important that the helper follows the dog and does not influence the search in any way. If your dog crosses the spot where you left the path, let her, as she will soon realise that the scent is gone. She will then probably begin to circle, find the scent again, and quickly discover you in your hiding place, in which case, remember to praise her as if she has performed a miracle.

In the next step the exercise is repeated; if possible, with a person known to your dog, and this time you are holding the leash. Of course, when to try this exercise always depends on the dog: we determine the way, the dog determines the speed. A very shy, sensitive dog will probably need to search for her own person more often to gain self-confidence. A more confident dog might be able to begin searching for strangers immediately, if she is easily motivated. The trainer's task is to correctly assess this situation. Avoid asking too much of your dog at all cost, especially at the beginning; start with a simple exercise and gradually increase the difficulty level. Conversely, make it challenging enough to avoid boredom.

If your dog has understood the purpose of the exercise, she should be incited but turned round to face away from the quarry. (This exercise is often used to demonstrate that the dog does actually use her nose.)

You could make it harder for your dog by entering the trail one or two metres from the side. This is an important preliminary exercise for later on, when your dog will have to decide in which direction to follow the trail. Right now the direction is determined by the person running away, but soon we will reach a stage where your dog will not need to see the person run away, and, even later, not even her handler will know which direction the quarry has taken, which should further boost your dog's self-confidence, as she will have to decide which direction to take. Of course, dogs are naturally well equipped to do this as their noses practically allow them to smell in stereo, just as we hear in stereo.

Now the trail becomes more and more difficult. First, we introduce a crossroad. The quarry takes a turning on the crossroad – without the dog watching – walks another 100 metres and hides, as before, in the forest.

Clear signals are necessary here to indicate the direction of the hiding place. We like to use different coloured clothes-pegs: for example, a certain colour means "this is the right way," whilst another means "I turned right after this and I am waiting in the hiding place." If there are enough trees with branches at eye level, this is a good way to mark the trail without interfering with the trail and your dog.

At one point during training I arrived at the following situation with my dog, Runa. Our quarry was not local and so I explained to her how to get to the hiding place. I was unsure about a part of the route she was to take, and told her to follow the path until she reached a small clearing with a raised hide at the end, where she was to turn right and then hide in the forest after a further 50 metres or so. Unfortunately, apart from a path I had forgotten, I also mixed up right and left at one point in my directions. Our quarry took the path I had forgotten existed, and, as there was a raised hide on that side as well, she turned right there. However, at the end she was nowhere near where I was expecting her to be! When I came across the forgotten path, I realised that she must have taken it. Runa followed that path, and almost certainly would have located her quarry had I not become so uncertain about her ability to complete the task that I projected this onto her and she stopped searching. In the end, we had to walk the entire forest with three search parties to find my helper, who didn't know where she was either!

This was a lesson we needed to be taught, and we have never laid out a trail without markings since. We also purchased walkie-talkies so that we always have a direct line to the quarry, which was a positive outcome to this story. Something that was not good was that it obviously made Runa very insecure – and could also have put her off searching permanently – she tried to do the right thing and I didn't trust her. Luckily, Runa does not hold a grudge because of that one occasion when I let her down.

It is important to always know which road the quarry has taken. If, in the interest of advanced training reasons, the handler is not supposed to know this, an accompanying assistant should be aware of the exact trail in order to reassure the handler in case of doubt.

Exactly as with trail searches without a person, as training proceeds, the trail becomes more and more difficult: for example, different angles should be included, preferably on crossroads. Something that should be taken into account is what effect wind has at a crossroad. Wind movement here can be extreme in some cases, which could mean that the scent is blown along a path that the quarry did not take. Let your dog follow the wind: she is supposed to discover for herself that she took a wrong turn, and she will, probably turning round at some point and working her way back to the original trail. It's extremely important to trust your dog here, because we do not know where the scent is. Maybe she can detect the scent very clearly but we are telling her it is the wrong direction, which is very likely to confuse her. Best to allow her to follow the wrong route for 50 metres or so; as long as she is well motivated to search, she will probably return by herself.

Also remember to include different ground surfaces. Have your quarry walk over tarmac, a gravel road, meadows, possibly very wet ground, or whatever else is available, and watch how your dog trails on various ground types. Does she have difficulty with any in particular? Does she, depending on the type of ground, hold her nose high or low? How do different weather conditions affect the search? All of these observations will help you to better understand your dog.

Always introduce her to new difficulties gradually, though remember that what can seem difficult to us, is really very simple for a dog. For example, if she is used to searching on pathways, a straight trail through the forest will be very easy for her, even though, to us, this would be a whole new challenge. For your dog, it is a relatively simple matter to distinguish what is probably the only human scent in the forest.

There are no limits to the tasks that a dog, or better still a dog/person team can be given to undertake. For example, the quarry could start out on the trail in the company of a whole group of people, only to leave them later on. Conversely, he or she could start out on their own and join a group of other people, whereupon your dog has to indicate which person is the quarry. In order to do this she must learn a type of indication that will unambiguously show who this is. It could be that she might bark at that person, jump in

Shakespeare follows the footprints precisely.

the air, sit or lie down in front of them, or something else. Consider the advantages and disadvantages and choose a method of indication suitable to your dog.

The hiding place could also be higher up, off the ground; for example, on a raised hide or in a tree. How will your dog deal with this, do you think? The scent will fall nicely to the ground, although there's a chance that it could drift away on the wind (see drawing, above), meaning that the scent is nowhere near the quarry. To make it easier for your dog, elevated hiding places should therefore only be used if there is little or no wind, at least initially.

The quarry could double-back and cross their own trail. Will your dog follow the original trail or begin following the more recent scent? (both of which can be considered correct). The dog that switches to the fresher trail appears to be really thinking about the situation; ie: the quarry is closer to this trail, so it would be a waste of energy to follow the older scent.

You can also ask your dog to follow trails that are older, and therefore not as fresh. Can she follow a two hour old trail? What happens if the trail is six hours old, or eight? A trail that is older than eight hours is usually called a 'cold' trail by hunters. With older trails than this, some breeds which have not been bred specifically to work with their noses may experience difficulty following them, although there are, for example, border collies capable of doing this without being bred to do so specifically. In my opinion, what is much more important than the breed is the trust that the handler has in their dog, as well as carefully structured training. So try this, even if you do not own a specially bred dog, such as a bloodhound. If you hit a limit in spite of careful and assiduous training, accept it!

There are many other challenges which will allow your dog to show off her abilities, and one of these is working with a scent pool. What is this? Well, a scent pool is a collection of scent of the person to be found.

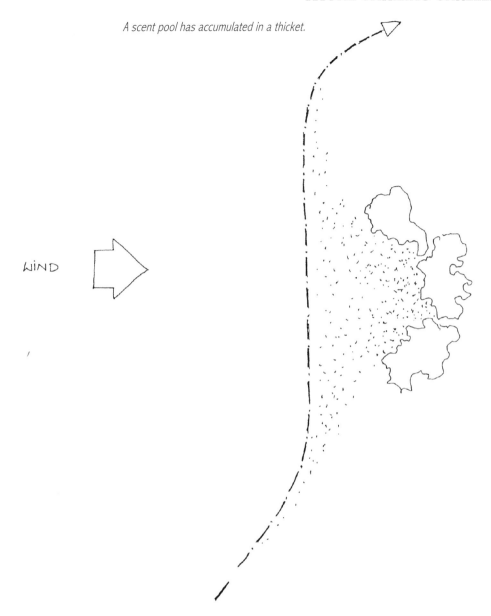

A scent pool has accumulated in a thicket.

WIND

In many ways, scent can be likened to water. If it gathers, for example in a hollow, the result is a scent pool; if a person remains in one place for a time, a lot of their scent gathers at that location, and this is also a scent pool, or maybe a scent cloud is a better description. Figuring out such a scent pool is the next big challenge for your dog.

Again, start slowly. Agree with the quarry the course to be taken. At some point — maybe at a bench but somewhere that is protected from the wind — he or she should sit down for five minutes and 'rest' before continuing to the hiding place, which should, initially, not be too far away from the resting place (of course, neither should it be too close, otherwise the two scent clouds could mix). Depending on terrain and wind, there should be at least fifty metres between the spot at which the quarry has rested and the eventual hiding place. Set your dog on the trail. How does she react when she gets to the scent pool or the scent cloud? Is she excited, maybe thinking she is getting closer to her target, as this spot smells so strongly of the person? So much scent may confuse her, as she would expect, in that case, to find the quarry. If possible, let her work it out for herself; she should realise that, in spite of the strong scent, the quarry is not there and will then locate the next part of the trail. If your dog finds the task too difficult, make it easier by having the quarry wait for one minute only at a certain spot so that the scent is not as strong; then increase this time gradually.

It is important that you learn to recognise when your dog enters such a scent pool. Practice correctly 'reading' your dog, as her behaviour will tell you what it is that she is smelling at that moment. You might find that she comes across a scent pool which has been generated by natural causes (see drawing, previous page). There may be situations where both the trailing abilities of your dog and your own intellect are needed to deal with questions such as where could the scent in the scent pool have originated? Does the wind come from above or below? What can I do to help my dog get back on the trail? These are tasks for a very advanced team and good communication between you and your dog are necessary to undertake them.

Once your dog is able to master a scent pool that is the result of a five minute break, you might ask your hider to move about in an area of, say, three by three metres during these five minutes, so that the entire area is filled with their scent. The hider should then leave this area at an arbitrary angle to the entry trail. Will the dog find the trail leading out of the area? How will she tackle this task, by concentrating mainly inside the area, or around the edge in an effort to locate the exit trail?

The first time you try this, you, as handler, must know which area has been used, and also learn how to read your dog. Once this works well, have others lay out trails for you that include tasks you and your dog have mastered in the past, but without telling you which these are, otherwise you might inadvertently signal this to your dog. Try and convey the message "I do not know where the trail is. You show me!" In difficult situations especially be patient and let your dog figure out the trail by herself. As I have already said, we cannot tell her where the scent is, but can try and refine communication between our dog and ourself via carefully and patiently planned exercises.

ADVANCED EXERCISES

TRAINING IN THE CITY

You have reached a point with your dog where you are seeking new challenges, curious to see what else your dog is capable of. I would like to present you with two further challenges: the first, searching in the city; and the second, the interrupted trail.

So, first the city. By now you should have had your dog search on tarmac many times already, but now lots more difficulties are added to this concept, such as cars and their exhaust fumes, many strange humans and whatever they leave behind them (food, sandwich leftovers, etc). Finally, wind movement between rows of houses is a problem in itself.

Having someone who can answer the questions of passers-by means you can concentrate on your dog and the trail.

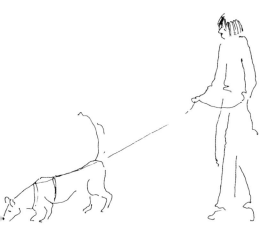

SMELLORAMA! Nose games for dogs

You and your dog should address these challenges one at a time. Begin in a quiet street with little vehicle or human traffic. Initially, you should know exactly where the person you are trying to find has gone, and chalk marks can sometimes help with this. This method is not infallible, however, as it may not always be possible to see the marks from the path that your dog is taking. For this reason, make sure you are clear about the route, or ensure you have a third person who knows the way. In any case, it's generally a good idea to have one or two helpers who could watch out for cars or answer the questions of passers-by, so that you can concentrate solely on working with your dog. Of course, if you have been able to infect other people with your enthusiasm for working with the dog's nose, then you can help each other!

At first, keep the trail short – a hundred metres (just over half a mile) or so; at this stage, it's not about your dog's endurance but his ability to learn a new task. Feel free to include one or two corners; for example, at crossroads. Watch carefully and observe how your dog reacts. Is he distracted by people, other scents, or maybe other dogs? If so, go back a few steps in training and try to include such a distraction in exercises that your dog is already familiar with. Ensure you are staying with the principle of only ever working on one new thing, with everything else in an exercise familiar to your dog. Also remember to reward him if he successfully masters this new exercise.

Slowly but steadily you can then make the city trails longer, and maybe try searching in different weather conditions. How well does your dog follow a trail that was laid on dry ground, but which has since been rained on? How does he cope with strong wind? Note down everything in your training diary as this will become a compendium of your experiences, from which you will be able draw ideas.

Also try to work with trails of different ages in the city. What are the results? Can your dog follow older trails in the city as well as in the field? Have you realised that a light

Even on concrete, a dog is easily able to follow his quarry's trail ...

... and when he finds her, lots of positive reinforcement is given in the form of praise and treats.

rain can make trailing easier for your dog? With very difficult tasks, consider helping him by making use of the morning dew.

THE INTERRUPTED TRAIL

A further, interesting challenge is the interrupted trail; interruptions of time as well as space.

Start with time interruption by halting the search at some point to take a break, removing your dog's harness to let him know that he can take a break now, too. Resuming the search, initially, you will have to present the scent again, although, once he understands the principle of interruption, he will continue on the right trail by himself as soon as he is given the opportunity to do so.

One example of a spatial interruption could be that the quarry walks in a stream for a while or crosses it completely. Dogs are surprisingly good at this type of trailing, and will use disturbed flora to follow the course of the quarry. If you have a chance to do so, use wider and wider streams. (This exercise is ideal for offering a little refreshment in the summer.)

What does your dog do if disturbed grass or other clues are not available? You could have him search up and down both banks of the stream until he rediscovers the trail, but, as with all other tasks, the principle that applies here is to lead him toward these tasks slowly. Initially it will be more than enough if the quarry walks through the water for two or three metres (two-and-a-half to three yards) only. If you succeed in adapting the exercise exactly to your dog's abilities, he will always participate with great enthusiasm. If you give him a task that is too difficult to master, however, he may feel that too much is being asked. Dogs react to this in different ways. Some abort the search altogether, others resort to marking more and more often (although this isn't common), and some assiduously follow the wrong scent. Watch out for these indicators that your dog is overchallenged, especially in the tasks detailed here. Be patient in training; it is so much easier to make progress if you take little steps.

Another way to interrupt a trail is to have a third person standing by with a bicycle at an agreed location. The quarry rides this for a few metres/yards (again, not too far initially), and then resumes walking. Exactly

In high temperatures, a stream can provide welcome refreshment.

as in crossing a stream, the trail does not stop completely, although it is very much altered in quality, and could be described as 'thinned out.' Challenges such as these can give new incentive to even experienced dogs, because just as a trail should never be too difficult to follow, it should also never be boring.

One way to achieve a completely interrupted trail is to include a drive in a car. This exercise needs some preparation as the car has to be left at some point on the planned trail by a third person. The best place to do this is on a tarmac rural road with little or no traffic.

Now the quarry walks to the car, travels for 100 metres (half a mile) or so, leaves the car and walks on. (Agree beforehand on the direction.) Don't forget to mark the spot where the trail is continued, or have a helper wait there to help you locate the right trail. When your dog loses the trail at the point where the quarry got into the car, simply walk along the road with him and, just before the point at which the trail resumes, encourage him to search. Observe him closely: at what point does he find the trail again? It may be that he is unable to pick up the scent again, in which case he will need to smell the marker again.

If he is successful in his attempt, you can increase the degree of difficulty with the help of two cars. The quarry travels approximately half a mile (100 metres). The second car with a driver is for you. Sit inside with your dog at the open window and encourage him to find the trail again. Ask the driver to drive very slowly, and sit on the side that you know the trail will continue along at some point. If you have reached this level of training you should be able to recognise the subtle hints your dog gives you when he believes he has found a trail. Leave the car at this point and let your dog follow the trail again.

For dogs trained to work in the city there is a further level in this exercise: your quarry could board a bus on the trail, after agreeing on the station that he or she will alight at. Follow with your dog, who will indubitably indicate at the station at which the quarry boarded the bus that the trail ends here. Take the next bus, get off at the agreed station and let your dog continue his search. During this trail, don't take your dog out of his harness; he is not taking a break, even if he is not actively searching during the ride. Once you have left the bus he has to try and relocate the trail by himself. If your dog masters this exercise, you could try disembarking at the wrong station. He won't be able to find a trail here and should tell you so with negative indication. Take the next bus and get off at the correct station to let him continue his work.

As you can see, there are virtually no limits to what you can plan for the training, which is what makes this type of work with your dog so interesting and exciting. You can never say "Well, now we can do everything," as you will always find new challenges to tackle.

CHANGES IN THE SCENT

Up until now we have used as a scent pattern something that our quarry has been wearing, which could either be presented to the dog in a plastic bag, or left lying on the ground at the start of the trail. Variations in this part of the exercise can make the tasks more challenging and/or exciting.

First, consider changing the size and material of the scent pattern; maybe work with smaller and smaller pieces of cloth. Objects like lighters or spectacles could also be used as scent patterns. And what about rings and earrings? In these cases, your dog must work with very little scent, but is able to cope with this as well! Amazing!

Once your dog has familiarised himself with all types of — possibly even very small — objects, you could also let him pick up scents from specific places. For example, the quarry may have sat in a beer garden and begun the trail from there, so locate the chair that the quarry (and no one else!) sat on and let your dog take in the scent there. Or you could show him the glass to pick up the scent, though don't be disappointed if he then indicates the waiter or the waitress: their scent is on the glass, too!

A good preliminary exercise in this respect would be to give your dog an object that has been held by two people, one of whom is present. In this way the dog can learn that *this* person does not need to be searched for, but the other one — whose scent is also on the object — *is* missing, and needs to be found.

You can also 'wrap up' scents and take them with you, in case you need them later on, though remember to wear disposable latex gloves when doing this. Your dog will probably also quickly understand that he's not required to find you, but avoid covering the scent to be found with your own. Take a sterile gauze, like the

The quarry's scent lingers on the chair; the hunt is on!

type found in first aid kits, and wipe over the outside of the beer glass. Put the gauze into the bag and you have a portable scent. In this way you can experiment and take scent from all sorts of surfaces. If this is an object that carries more than one scent, it would be preferable if the other people were present so that your dog understands that they are not the quarry. It is not our intention to confuse our dog, but to become more flexible with our scent patterns. Again, you will be amazed and fascinated by the initially unbelievable feats our dogs are able to perform.

Failure — in most cases — is usually the result of bad communication. Be aware of this and use the knowledge to set lessons that your dog can understand. With the necessary perception of the normal behaviour and learning patterns of your dog, together you can achieve remarkable things.

I hope my book has given you the information and, more importantly, the enthusiasm to work with your dog in this way, which is especially suitable for people who are willing to learn from their dog and who aren't under any illusion that they need to teach their dog how to smell! Please note, though, that serious searching — as applied, for example, by rescue dogs — requires much more specialist knowledge and training than this book is intended to provide.

Almost every dog likes to sniff and snuffle, and is able to accomplish remarkable feats. Apart from being an activity with a purpose, scenting can also improve our relationship with our dog, and communication between us, which, in turn, will have positive effects on other areas of our lives together.

Enjoy!

BIBLIOGRAPHY

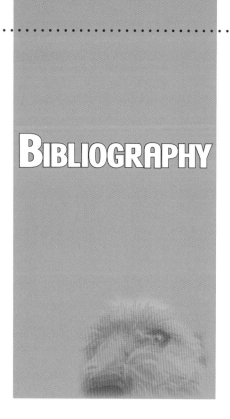

Keep sniffing: more nose games for dogs
Viviane Theby & Michaela Hares. Kynos Verlag, 2004
More fun and exciting ways for your dog to use her
nose and brain. Who knows, maybe she will even find
Granddad's hearing aid ...

Scent and the Scenting Dog
William G Syrotuck, Barkleigh Productions, 2000
Development of scents in detail

Practical scent training for dogs
Lue Button. Alpine Publications, 1990
Teaching your dog different searching methods

Click 'n' Sniff
Deborah A Jones PhD. Howln Moon Press, 2001
How to use a clicker to teach scenting

*Hundeschule: Hundgerecht lernen ohne Stress.
Motivation und Belohnung statt Strafe. Erfolgreich
erziehen Schritt für Schritt (Dog school: motivation
and reward instead of punishment and learning
without stress)*
Viviane Theby
Kynos Verlag, 2002
The teaching theories behind kind dog training,
which every dog owner should be familiar with

Dogs in Rescue Services
Andrea von Buddenbrock
Kynos Verlag, 2003
Training and usage of dogs inn rescue situations

Notes ...

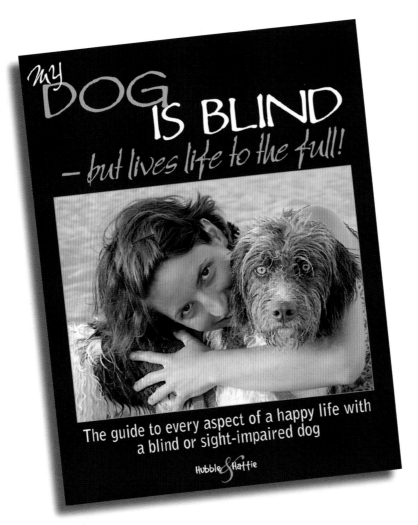

★ Diagnosis ★ Eye problems ★ Socialisation ★ In the house and garden ★ Calming signals ★ Stress ★ Basic commands ★ Off-lead ★ Fun and games ★ Smellorama! scenting/nosework ★ Integration with other dogs ★ Tricks ★ Tips for training ★ Closing thoughts

Paperback with flaps. 80 pages. 220mm tall x 170mm. 40 pictures, 20 in colour. ISBN 978-1-845842-91-8. UPC 6-36847-04291-2. £9.99 UK/$19.95 USA

★ A wheelchair is no barrier to dog ownership! ★ Benefits of dog ownership ★ Positive effects on state of mind ★ Basic considerations ★ Physical restrictions ★ Caring for your dog ★ Walkin' the dog ★ Clothing ★ Special equipment ★ Suitable breeds ★ Dog size and temperament ★ Ability/selection/acquisition ★ Training for a special life ★ Walking behaviour ★ Night-time excursions ★ Winter-time ★ The law, you and your dog ★ On tour ★ Wheelchair, dog and competition ★ Water sport ★ Your dog and travelling ★ Ideas for trips ★ Wheelchair, dog and traffic ★ General problems ★ Where next? ★ Appendix

Paperback with flaps. 96 pages.
220mm tall x 170mm. 18 colour pictures, 9 mono.
ISBN 978-1-845842-92-5. UPC 6-36847-04292-9
£12.99 UK/$24.95 USA

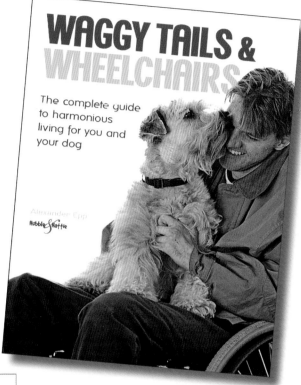

★ Recognise your dog's personality ★ A world of emotions ★ Emotions can be guided ★ A dog's senses ★ How dogs learn and reason ★ Playful training ★ How does a dog see itself? ★ Recognising skills and helping them develop ★ Sleeping and dreaming ★ The daily mental workout ★ Learning exercises with 'zing' ★ Exercises to keep your dog fit ★ Tricky tests of logic ★ Memory training ★ Tips and information

Hardback. 96 pages. 220mm tall x 165mm.
76 colour pictures.
ISBN 978-1-845840-72-3. UPC 6-36847-04072-7
£9.99

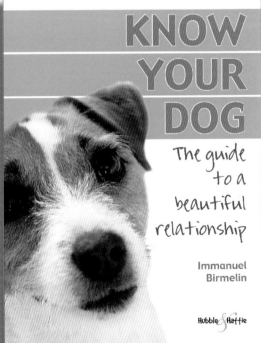

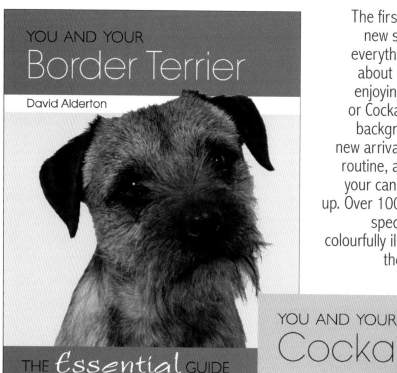

Gentle Dog Care

Gentle Dog Care

the complete **massage** manual

Julia Robertson

The first book in another new series, Gentle Dog Care will guide you in looking after your best friend in the kindest, most canine-friendly way possible!

Introduction ★ How your dog works ★ Using your vet ★ How does massage work? ★ The basic techniques ★ How to massage your dog ★ Massage & muscular health from puppy to veteran ★ Post-operative & post-injury dog ★ Other techniques

Paperback. 205 x 205mm. 128 pages. 100 colour photos.
ISBN 978-1-845843-22-9. UPC 6-36847-04322-3. £12.99

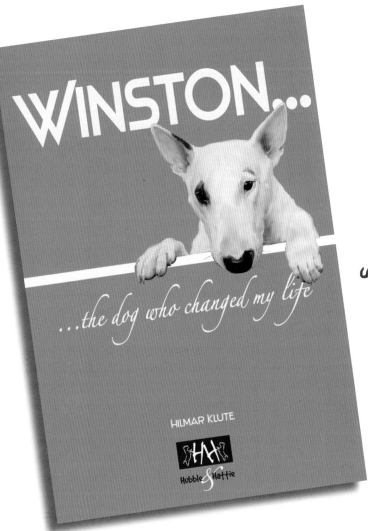

As featured in *The Sunday Express*, this is the captivating story of how, abandoned to his fate in a cemetery, Winston finds his forever home in a very unexpected way!

★ Winston was a puppy, found abandoned and tethered to a gravestone in a city cemetery ★ The true story of how a non-dog lover unexpectedly became a dog owner ★ Experience the strange, new and unfamiliar world of dogs and their owners from a complete newcomer's perspective ★ A charming and irreverent story ★ Reveals some surprising truths about the relationship between dog and man ★ Casts a critical eye over the professional 'dog whisperer' ★ Will appeal to many kinds of reader: those who know nothing about dogs, those who love dogs, and perhaps even those who cannot stand dogs!

Hardback & jacket. 160 pages. 180mm tall x 120mm. Drawings throughout. ISBN 978-1-845842-74-1. UPC 6-36847-04274-5. £9.99 UK/$17.95 USA